# Information Retrieval Evaluation

# Synthesis Lectures on Information Concepts, Retrieval, and Services

Editor
**Gary Marchionini,** *University of North Carolina, Chapel Hill*

Synthesis Lectures on Information Concepts, Retrieval, and Services is edited by Gary Marchionini of the University of North Carolina. The series will publish 50- to 100-page publications on topics pertaining to information science and applications of technology to information discovery, production, distribution, and management. The scope will largely follow the purview of premier information and computer science conferences, such as ASIST, ACM SIGIR, ACM/IEEE JCDL, and ACM CIKM. Potential topics include, but not are limited to: data models, indexing theory and algorithms, classification, information architecture, information economics, privacy and identity, scholarly communication, bibliometrics and webometrics, personal information management, human information behavior, digital libraries, archives and preservation, cultural informatics, information retrieval evaluation, data fusion, relevance feedback, recommendation systems, question answering, natural language processing for retrieval, text summarization, multimedia retrieval, multilingual retrieval, and exploratory search.

Information Retrieval Evaluation

Donna Harman

ISBN:978-3-031-01148-1   paperback
ISBN:978-3-031-02276-0   ebook

DOI 10.1007/978-3-031-02276-0

A Publication in the Springer series
*SYNTHESIS LECTURES ON INFORMATION CONCEPTS, RETRIEVAL, AND SERVICES*

Lecture #19
Series Editor: Gary Marchionini, *University of North Carolina, Chapel Hill*
Series ISSN
Synthesis Lectures on Information Concepts, Retrieval, and Services
Print 1947-945X   Electronic 1947-9468

# Information Retrieval Evaluation

Donna Harman

National Institute of Standards and Technology

*SYNTHESIS LECTURES ON INFORMATION CONCEPTS, RETRIEVAL, AND SERVICES #19*

# ABSTRACT

Evaluation has always played a major role in information retrieval, with the early pioneers such as Cyril Cleverdon and Gerard Salton laying the foundations for most of the evaluation methodologies in use today. The retrieval community has been extremely fortunate to have such a well-grounded evaluation paradigm during a period when most of the human language technologies were just developing. This lecture has the goal of explaining where these evaluation methodologies came from and how they have continued to adapt to the vastly changed environment in the search engine world today. The lecture starts with a discussion of the early evaluation of information retrieval systems, starting with the Cranfield testing in the early 1960s, continuing with the Lancaster "user" study for MEDLARS, and presenting the various test collection investigations by the SMART project and by groups in Britain.

The emphasis in this chapter is on the how and the why of the various methodologies developed. The second chapter covers the more recent "batch" evaluations, examining the methodologies used in the various open evaluation campaigns such as TREC, NTCIR (emphasis on Asian languages), CLEF (emphasis on European languages), INEX (emphasis on semi-structured data), etc. Here again the focus is on the how and why, and in particular on the evolving of the older evaluation methodologies to handle new information access techniques. This includes how the test collection techniques were modified and how the metrics were changed to better reflect operational environments. The final chapters look at evaluation issues in user studies–the interactive part of information retrieval, including a look at the search log studies mainly done by the commercial search engines. Here the goal is to show, via case studies, how the high-level issues of experimental design affect the final evaluations.

# KEYWORDS

evaluation, test collections, information retrieval, Cranfield paradigm, TREC

# Contents

# Acknowledgments

No book is written by one person, and I am grateful to all the writers that came before me for their meticulous attention to detail and careful documentation of their methodologies and results. I am also very grateful for the many discussions with members of the information retrieval community over the years as we jointly debated evaluation. The Retrieval Group at NIST (especially Ian Soboroff and Paul Over) and Chris Buckley patiently listened to me and then told me where I was wrong, and for this I am very beholden for getting the details correct in this lecture. Emily Morse of NIST did a preliminary review of Chapter 3 and assured me that I had properly documented an area that is not my strength.

A very special thanks to Stephen Robertson for several critical items. He helped to gather the older material from the British Library and got permission for me to scan this for public consumption. Having access to all these older reports, plus some that Doug Oard was able to borrow from the University of Maryland gave me the material I needed. Stephen was also a preliminary reviewer of Chapter 1 on the early history and I am grateful for his helpful comments.

A second very very special thanks to Ellen Voorhees, not only for many good discussions, but also for an extremely careful review of Chapter 2, making sure that I did get it right and that the (often) subtle issues in TREC were properly recorded.

And finally I am very grateful to the reviewers of the entire lecture, Mark Smucker and John Tait, who not only caught many little errors, but highlighted areas that needed more work or better explanations. I appreciate the time they took to read it, to write helpful comments, and to help me think further about some important issues.


Donna Harman
May 2011

CHAPTER 1

# Introduction and Early History

## 1.1 INTRODUCTION

Information retrieval systems can be evaluated for many reasons, such as which search engine to use personally, what commercial system to buy, or how to improve the user-friendliness of a system interface. This lecture is not about any of these types of evaluation, but rather about the measurement of how well a system is doing in retrieval, and about how to develop testing that will enable system researchers to better understand what is happening inside the system. The emphasis in the entire lecture is on making sure that the methodologies used for testing actually measure what the researchers *think* is being measured, and that any biases in evaluation can be recognized.

The first chapter discusses the early evaluation of information retrieval systems, starting with the Cranfield testing in the early 1960s, continuing with the Lancaster "user" study for MEDLARS, and presenting the various test collection investigations by the SMART project and by groups in Britain. The emphasis in this chapter is on the how and the why of the various methodologies developed. One component of the methodologies is the measures of effectiveness, i.e., the metrics that were used, and whereas there is some discussion of these metrics, readers are generally referred to more complete presentations elsewhere. It should be noted that many of the older references for this chapter are now available online. Readers particularly interested in the early history should also see [134, 147, 167].

The second chapter covers the more recent "batch" evaluations, examining the methodologies used in the various open evaluation campaigns such as TREC, NTCIR (emphasis on Asian languages), CLEF (emphasis on European languages), INEX (emphasis on semi-structured data), etc. Here again the focus is on the how and why, and in particular on the evolving of the older evaluation methodologies to handle new information access techniques. This includes how the test collection techniques were modified and how the metrics were changed to better reflect operational environments. The chapter also contains some advice on how to build a test collection. Most of the references from this chapter are also available online.

The third chapter looks at evaluation issues in user studies–the interactive part of information retrieval. The chapter starts with a short review of evaluation in early user studies, such as those of indexers and search intermediaries, followed by a discussion of the evaluation experiences in the interactive track in TREC. The final section is a look at recent user studies, including the search log studies mainly done by the commercial search engines. Here the goal is to show, via case studies, how the high-level issues of experimental design affect the final evaluations.

The fourth and final chapter presents some thoughts on how to actually do an experiment, pulling together some of the ideas from earlier chapters. Additionally there is discussion of some very recent issues in evaluation, both in methodology and in metrics, and a look ahead at some future challenges.

## 1.2    THE CRANFIELD TESTS

The Cranfield paradigm (developed by Cyril Cleverdon) is often cited as a "standard" for information retrieval evaluation. But what exactly is this paradigm, where did it come from, and what are the critical components of it? (To read Cleverdon's own account of the Cranfield tests and their background, see his acceptance speech for the 1991 SIGIR award [53].)

There were actually two separate tests conducted by Cleverdon, Librarian of the College of Aeronautics, Cranfield, England and his staff. The first, Cranfield I running from 1958 to 1962 [48, 49], was specifically designed to test four manual indexing (classification) methods. It is hard today to imagine the information access methods that existed at that time—text was not available electronically, and information could only be found by "word-of-mouth" or specialist librarians, who mainly used manually produced, massive indexes to publications. Examples of these systems still exist today, such as the Medical Subject Index, or the Engineering Index.

There had been a huge increase in the volume of scientific papers after World War II and scientists were forced to rely on these indexes to keep current. But these indexes were very expensive to create and there was much contention as to which type of indexing system to use. An editorial [1] called for serious evaluation of these various competing indexing (classification) systems: "Cautious and searching evaluation of all experimental results is essential in rating the efficiency of documentation systems. May the age old controversies that arose from the conventional concepts of classification not be reborn in the mechanized searching systems of the future."

Cleverdon took this editorial as encouragement, and after presenting a paper in Detroit in June 1955, was invited to submit a proposal to the National Science Foundation to create such an evaluation. This proposal was funded and work started in April of 1958. The proposal summarized the various factors that needed to be considered, including the number and type of documents which were to be indexed, the indexing systems, the indexer's subject knowledge of the documents and familiarity with the indexing system, and the type of question to be searched. It also proposed to examine the overall efficiency, such as the time cost to prepare the index and to locate required information, and the probability of producing the required answer while minimizing the irrelevant answers ("noise").

The 18,000 papers and reports to be indexed were from the field of aerodynamics (obviously readily available). The four indexing systems tested were an alphabetical subject catalogue, a faceted classification scheme, the Universal Decimal Classification and the Uniterm system of co-ordinate indexing, representing the dominant types of manual indexing schemes in vogue. There were 3 indexers with different levels of experience in the subject matter. Experience using the different indexing systems was controlled by careful rotation among the various systems throughout the testing (similar to the Latin Square designs used today). Indexing was done in rotation of blocks of 100 documents, with one system used as the primary index (to be created in an average of 16 minutes per document) and then the indexing for the other three systems finished in much shorter times (the time allowed for indexing was an additional control). It took two years of work to finish this indexing project, with many difficulties encountered along the way (such as major indexer fatigue).

Whereas this first stage of Cranfield 1 was working within a somewhat familiar paradigm, there was little to guide decisions for the second stage (the searching). One previous test, known as the ASTIA-Uniterm test, had been done in 1953, but never fully documented [76]. In this case there had been two teams, each using one of two indexing methods for 15,000 documents. About 93 real user questions were then searched by each team using their index. The end result was that there was no agreement between the teams as to the relevance of the documents and each team generated their own report based on their results!

Cleverdon wanted to avoid this relevance trap, but also wanted to make sure the results would pass significance testing. He estimated that as many as 1,600 questions would be needed, with full searching then done on the four different indexes. This seemed impossible and therefore he decided on what is known today as *known–item searching*, i.e., finding the one document (which he called the "source document") that was guaranteed to be relevant for a given question.

It was critical that the evaluation mirror a true operational setting, in particular that of a researcher searching for a given document in the 18,000 indexed documents. Cleverdon carefully constructed the questions by asking authors of documents in his indexed collection to select some of their documents and then "frame a question that could be satisfactorily answered by that document". In all he received 1500 such questions, which were then subsetted into random batches for various stages of testing. As a final check, he submitted the first batch of 400 questions to a panel who verified that these were indeed typical user questions (only one question was discarded).

The searching process required using each index to manually search for the documents, recording the search time and the success (or failure) of the search. The results–the search failed an average of 35% of the time, with no significant differences among the indexing systems. All of the failures were due to "human indexing error", which did not significantly differ across the indexers.

Whereas the results seemed inconclusive on the surface, Cleverdon was able to discover the real problem simply because of the huge amount of data that was examined in the failure analysis. The issue was not the specific indexing system used, but rather the actual content descriptors that were used for each document. Were the descriptors multiple terms or single terms and how many descriptors were included? More descriptors (exhaustive indexing) lead to better recall (generally), but at the expense of precision (called "relevance" up to 1964). What about weighting the indexing terms, or what he called syntactic indexing involving a method of showing relationships between terms? The problem of how to select content descriptors for indexing, and an increasing interest in evaluation issues, led Cleverdon to continue his investigations in the Cranfield 2 (1962-1966) project [51, 52].

What was learned in Cranfield 1 about the evaluation methodology? Because of the multiple partitionings of the documents for indexing and searching, and the fact that results were similar across these batches, Cleverdon realized that far fewer documents were needed for testing. This was verified by a small experiment by Cleverdon and Jean Aitchinson at Western Reserve University [3] where only 1000 documents were used in similar testing. The creation of the test questions by the use of source documents seemed to work well, avoiding the need for relevance judging (and its inherent instability).

Cleverdon applied these ideas in his design for Cranfield 2, deciding to aim for about 1200 documents and 300 questions. He felt that it was critical to first build the test collection (documents, questions, and relevance judgments), and then do the experiments on the indexing and searching. Additionally it was critical to carefully model his users in building this test collection. The documents needed to be ones they would naturally search, the questions needed to reflect ones they might ask, and the relevance judgments needed to mirror the type of judgments researchers would make for documents they examined in the search process.

He again used the source document method to gather questions, but modified it in order to locate all the relevant documents for a given question rather than just the one source document. The titles of 271 papers published in 1962 on the subject of high speed aerodynamics and the theory of aircraft structures were sent to their authors, along with a listing of up to 10 papers that were cited by these papers. The following instructions were also sent to these authors.

1. State the basic problem, in the form of a search question, which was the reason for the research being undertaken leading to the paper, and also give not more than three supplemental questions that arose in the course of the work, and which were, or might have been, put to an information service.

2. Assess the relevance of each of the submitted list of papers which had been cited as references, in relation to each of the questions given. The assessment is to be based on the following scale of five definitions:

   (a) References which are a complete answer to the question.

   (b) References of a high degree of relevance, the lack of which either would have made the research impractical or would have resulted in a considerable amount of extra work.

   (c) References which were useful, either as general background to the work or as suggesting methods of tackling certain aspects of the work.

   (d) References of minimal interest, for example, those that have been included from an historical viewpoint

   (e) References of no interest

There were 173 useful forms returned, with an average of 3.5 questions per form. The document collection was built by merging the 173 source documents with their cited documents (those that had been previously sent to the authors for judgments), and 209 similar documents, for a total of 1400 documents.

The next stage involved getting relevance assessments for all of the 1400 documents. A smaller set of 361 questions were selected based on their grammatical correctness and on a minimal number of known relevant from the authors. Five graduate students spent the summer of 1963 making preliminary (and liberal) judgments for these 361 questions against all 1400 documents. These judgments were then conveyed to the question authors for a final decision, based on the five graded levels of judging used previously. Judgments were returned for 279 of the questions, although for various reasons usually only 221 of them were used in testing (compound questions were removed for example).

At this point, the test collection was built and experimentation could begin. Note that the goal of Cranfield 2 was to examine in more depth the various properties of index methodologies. Rather than selecting specific indexing systems as in Cranfield 1, Cleverdon and his team wanted to build a "complete" set of index variations for each document and then perform manual experiments using these variations, in this case 33 different index types (see Figure 1.1 for the complete set). The primary performance scores, however, would come from the results of searching using these various index types.

The experimental setup was as follows: each experiment was defined by a series of rules that specified which of the many possible combinations of variables would be used. The searchers then manually followed these rules using coded cards stored in what was known as the "Beehive". So for example, an experiment could involve one specific type of index and a series of *precision device* "runs" using different levels of co-ordination (the Boolean "anding" of terms or concepts during the search process) on a per question basis. For "run 1" of that experiment, each question was indexed by the specific index type being investigated, all index terms from that question were "anded", and the documents meeting that criterion were manually retrieved. This resulted in a single score. The experiment continued with "run 2" which had one less index term used, and so on until only one index term was used for searching.

Cranfield 2 did not emphasize the searching; in general only different co-ordination levels were used. The main focus was the indexing, which was done manually using three basic types of indexing languages: single terms, simple concepts, and controlled terms. On top of this basic structure there were what Cleverdon called *recall devices*, such as the use of the (stemmed) *word forms*, and the use of synonyms and/or hierarchies from a thesaurus. There were also precision devices such as weighting in addition to the co-ordination level searching.

The documents were first indexed at the simple concept level, i.e., "terms which in isolation are weak and virtually useless as retrieval handles were given the necessary context; such terms as 'high', 'number', 'coefficient', etc.". These simple concepts were manually assigned weights based on their importance to document: 9/10 for the main general theme of the document, 7/8 for a major subsidiary theme, and 5/6 for a minor subsidiary theme. The simple concepts could then be broken into their single terms, with weights assigned to these terms based on the concept weight

| ORDER | NORMALISED RECALL | | | INDEXING LANGUAGE |
|---|---|---|---|---|
| 1 | 65.82 | I-3 | Single terms. | Word forms |
| 2 | 65.23 | I-2 | Single terms. | Synonyms |
| 3 | 65.00 | I-1 | Single terms. | Natural Language |
| 4 | 64.47 | I-6 | Single terms. | Synonyms, word forms, quasi-synonyms |
| 5 | 64.41 | I-8 | Single terms. | Hierarchy second stage |
| 6 | 64.05 | I-7 | Single terms. | Hierarchy first stage |
| 7= | 63.05 | I-5 | Single terms. | Synonyms.   Quasy-synonyms |
| 7= | 63.05 | II-11 | Simple concepts. | Hierarchical and alphabetical selection |
| 9 | 62.88 | II-10 | Simple concepts. | Alphabetical second second stage selection |
| 10= | 61.76 | III-1 | Controlled terms. | Basic terms |
| 10= | 61.76 | III-2 | Controlled terms. | Narrower terms |
| 12 | 61.17 | I-9 | Single terms. | Hierarchy third stage |
| 13 | 60.94 | IV-3 | Abstracts. | Natural language |
| 14 | 60.82 | IV-4 | Abstracts. | Word forms |
| 15 | 60.11 | III-3 | Controlled terms. | Broader terms |
| 16 | 59.76 | IV-2 | Titles. | Word forms |
| 17 | 59.70 | III-4 | Controlled terms. | Related terms |
| 18 | 59.58 | III-5 | Controlled terms. | Narrower and broader and terms |
| 19 | 59.17 | III-6 | Controlled terms. | Narrower, broader and related terms |
| 20 | 58.94 | IV-1 | Titles. | Natural language |
| 21 | 57.41 | II-15 | Simple concepts. | Complete combination |
| 22 | 57.11 | II-9 | Simple concepts. | Alphabetical first stage selection |
| 23 | 55.88 | II-13 | Simple concepts. | Complete species and superordinate |
| 24 | 55.76 | II-8 | Somple concepts. | Hierarchical selection |
| 25 | 55.41 | II-12 | Simple concepts. | Complete species |
| 26 | 55.05 | II-5 | Simple concepts. | Selected species and superordinate |
| 27 | 53.88 | II-7 | Simple concepts. | Selected coordinate and collateral |
| 28 | 53.52 | II-3 | Simple concepts. | Selected species |
| 29 | 52.47 | II-14 | Simple concepts. | Complete collateral |
| 30 | 52.05 | II-4 | Simple concepts. | Superordinate |
| 31 | 51.82 | II-6 | Simple concepts. | Selected coordinate |
| 32 | 47.41 | II-2 | Simple concepts. | Synonyms |
| 33 | 44.64 | II-1 | Simple concepts. | Natural language |

FIGURE 8.1 T    ORDER OF EFFECTIVENESS BASED ON NORMALISED
RECALL FOR 33 CRANFIELD INDEX LANGUAGES
(AVERAGE OF NUMBERS)

**Figure 1.1:** The 33 variations of indexing used in Cranfield 2.

and the indexer's view of the term's concreteness and potency. The controlled terms were created by translating the simple concepts into the vocabulary of the Thesaurus of Engineering Terms of the Engineers Joint Council.

Chapter 5 of [52] gives the details of this indexing, including tables showing that there were 3094 unique single terms in the 1400 documents, with an average postings per document of 31.3 single terms (with any weights), 25.2 single terms with weights 7/10 and 12.9 single terms with weights 9/10, giving three levels of exhaustivity of indexing. The manual document indexing was done on the full documents, but as a contrast, and as a way of creating two more levels of exhaustivity, the titles only and the titles plus the abstracts were "automatically" indexed. The details of this are sketchy in the report; however, it is likely that any of the terms that had been declared single terms (3094 of them) and were contained in the abstracts/titles were considered to the automatic indexes of these, including multiple occurrences of the same term. This gave an average of 7 single terms to the titles and 60 single terms to the abstracts plus titles. Figure 1.1 gives the 33 types of index schemes, including the performance ranking of the various schemes using types of scoring that will be described next.

There had been a lot of discussion previously about metrics, centering around the well-known categories shown in Table 1.1. Cleverdon decided to use the "Recall Ratio" defined as $a/(a+c)$, and the "Precision Ratio" $a/(a+b)$. These had been used by Perry [128] and called the Recall Factor and the Pertinency Factor, respectively. Other names previously used for the recall ratio were the sensitivity or the hit ratio, with the precision ratio known as the relevance ratio, the pertinency factor or the acceptance rate (see [147] for more on the history of metrics). Cleverdon liked both the simplicity of recall and precision and the fact that they directly described a user's experience and therefore chose these over more complex formulas such as those suggested by Bourne, Farradane, Vickery, etc.

It should be noted that for each of the 221 questions the recall and precision ratios measured a *single* point for each run in an experiment. Using the example experiment described earlier, each of the co-ordinate levels would generate a single recall and a precision point, e.g., co-ordinating 5 terms yields 28% recall at 29% precision, 4 terms gives 40% recall at 12% precision, and using only one term gives 95% recall at 1% precision. These could be plotted on a recall/precision curve looking much like today's curves, but with each point representing a single experiment as opposed to one curve for each experiment.

There were also issues about how to average these points across the full set of questions. The Cranfield experiments usually worked with the grand total figures of the relevant and retrieved across all of the questions, i.e., sum up the total number of relevant retrieved and the total number of documents retrieved for all questions and then divide by the number of questions. This today is called the micro-averaging method and was the simplest to calculate (remember they were not using computers). Cleverdon was aware of the problems with this method; in that, questions with many relevant documents skewed the results, and therefore he did some experimentation with per question ratios (known as macro-averaging).

**Table 1.1:** Possible categories of documents in searching.

|  | Relevant | Non-relevant |  |
|---|---|---|---|
| Retrieved | a | b | a + b |
| Not Retrieved | c | d | c + d |
|  | a + c | b + d | a + b + c + d = N |

It soon became apparent that there was too much to do; several subsets of the collection were then used. In particular, the Cranfield 200 was created using 42 questions on aerodynamics, along with 198 of their relevant documents (but not the source documents for these questions). This then created a new problem because experiments done on different subsets could not be directly compared; there were radically different ratios of relevant/non-relevant documents for the 42 questions in the 200 vs. the 1400. The "generality" measure, the ratio of number of relevant documents to the total number of documents in the collection, was defined as $(a + c)/(a + b + c + d)$ and used, along with the "fallout" ratio $b/(b + d)$ which measured the experiments ability to avoid retrieving non-relevant documents.

So what were the results of this huge set of experiments? Figure 1.1 copied from Figure 8.1T in [51], lists the order of effectiveness of 33 different "index languages". The scoring is based on a simulated ranking method (see Chapter 5 in [51] for details) coming from the SMART project and using the normalized recall metric (see Section 1.4). The top seven indexing languages used only single terms, with the very best results found using the word forms (stems) of these single terms. Cleverdon summarized his reaction to these results on the first page of his conclusions [51].

"Quite the most astonishing and seemingly inexplicable conclusion that arises from the project is that the single term index languages are superior to any other type. ....This conclusion is so controversial and so unexpected that it is bound to throw considerable doubt on the methods which have been used to obtain these results, and our first reaction was to doubt the evidence. A complete recheck has failed to reveal any discrepancies, and unless one is prepared to say that the whole test conception is so much at fault that the results are completely distorted, then there is no other course except to attempt to explain the results which seem to offend against every canon on which we were trained as librarians."

Of course there was a great furor from the community and arguments over the Cranfield methodology were fierce [84, 130, 171]. These mostly centered on the use of source documents to generate questions (as opposed to real questions) and on the definitions of relevancy. Whereas some of these came from community rejection of the experimental conclusions, many were reasonable objections for the Cranfield paradigm (although the general consensus was that the experimental results were valid).

There were two very important outcomes from Cranfield 2 for the field of information retrieval. First it had been shown *conclusively* that using the actual terms in a document, as opposed to any type of pre-determined combination or alteration of these terms (such as the simple concepts), resulted in the best searching performance. Whereas the single terms at the top seven ranks were the result of manual indexing (specific terms being picked), even the "automatic" indexing of abstracts and titles at rank 13 beat out the simple concepts. This result was not only astonishing to the library community, but gave the new computer science community, such as Gerard Salton and the SMART project, the justification to move from experiments in indexing to more detailed experiments in searching.

The second important outcome was the Cranfield paradigm for evaluation. Today this is generally taken to mean the use of a static test collection of documents, questions, and relevance judgments, often with standard recall and precision metrics. But there are two other subtle components that Cleverdon was insistent on. The first was the careful modeling of the task being tested by the test collection. So his collection of scientific documents, his selection of "users" (via the source document method) that would heavily use this collection, and his careful definition of relevance based on how these *particular* users might judge documents were critical pieces of the Cranfield paradigm. The other component was his strict separation of the building of the test collection from the experimentation itself. This was done to avoid problems in earlier experiments, and one can only wonder if his results would have been so clear if he had not followed this principle. Both of these latter components are largely forgotten today, but need to be further examined in light of the various current projects based on Cranfield paradigm.

## 1.3    THE MEDLARS EVALUATION

It is interesting to contrast the Cranfield work with the other major study that took place during 1966 and 1967–the MEDLARS (Medical Literature Analysis and Retrieval System) evaluation [115]. By way of background, there were approximately 700,000 indexed citations online for medicine by 1966, with 2400 scientific journals being indexed using a huge (7000 categories at that time) controlled vocabulary thesaurus (the Medical Subject Headings, or MeSH). The citations were growing at around 200,000 per year, and the National Library of Medicine offered a search service using search intermediaries for these citations.

The Library asked F.W. Lancaster to do an evaluation of this search service, with the following goals: to study the user requirements, to find out how well the service was meeting those requirements, to identify factors affecting performance, and to suggest improvements. The evaluation was also required to create a test collection, with documents, requests/questions, indexing, search formulations and relevance assessments, and Cleverdon was an advisor.

The specific factors to be measured were the coverage of MEDLARS, the recall and precision of the searches, the response times, the format of the results, and the amount of effort needed by users. It should be noted that these factors depended on many of the variables that Cleverdon had already been investigating, such as inter-indexer performance, the necessary level of exhaustivity of indexing, and the adequacy of the indexing language (the MeSH thesaurus). But because this was an operational test, there was specific interest in the users, such as what were their requirements with respect to recall and precision, what were the best modes of interaction between the users and search intermediaries, and what was the effect of the response times?

This emphasis on the users meant that the user "population" had to be picked carefully. Rather than using a random sample of requests, the study identified a number of specific user groups who agreed to cooperate during the evaluation program. These were groups that were likely to submit enough requests during the testing period, to put in the types of requests that would be representative of the whole user population, to come from different types of organizations, and to have close enough interaction with the search services so that interactions could be carefully studied. Twenty-one groups were selected, including seven academic organizations, five U.S. government health organizations, two pharmaceutical companies, five clinical organizations such as hospitals, and two U.S. regulatory agencies.

These groups agreed to participate and 410 requests were collected between August 1966 and July 1967. Note that the individual requesters (users) did not know about the testing until their requests were submitted, at which time they were asked if they were willing to be part of this test. So the requests were real information needs. These requests were then searched in a normal manner (although the searchers did know these were test requests) and the citations that were found were returned to the user (copies of the entire documents).

In addition to this normal procedure, these users were asked to fill in two types of forms. The first type asked for "relevance" assessment of a subset of the documents that had been returned. Between 25 and 30 documents were in this subset, randomly selected from the full set of documents that had been returned to the user. For each document the user was asked first if they knew of this document's existence, and then to pick one of three relevance categories: "of major value to me in relation to my information need", "of minor value", and "of no value". They were also asked to explain why.

These assessment forms allowed the computation of a precision ratio, in which the number of documents marked relevant was divided by the number in the judged subset (not the number in the full MEDLARS collection). Because these documents had been picked at random from the full returned list, it was assumed that this precision ratio could be extrapolated as the precision for this request if the whole list had been examined. There was also a novelty ratio, calculated as the percentage of the relevant returned that had NOT been previously known to the user.

But this did not address recall, and it would have been impossible to judge all of the MEDLARS citations for each request. The recall was estimated by building what was known as the "recall" base. Each of the users was asked to fill in a second type of form after they submitted their request. In this form they were asked to list all known relevant documents that had been published since July 1963 (when the MEDLARS citation service had started), and to list relevancy (presumably major or minor) for each of those documents. A quick glance at the full results shown in Appendix 4 of [115] shows that most forms listed well less that 10 known documents, with a likely median of around 5 (it is not clear from the report what this number actually is). For about 80% of the searches, additional documents were found using manual searching (usually by NLM staff) using non-NLM tools to avoid test bias. These additional documents were also submitted to the user for relevance assessment (mixed in with the other citations that had been returned). The recall ratio could then be calculated based on the number of relevant (either known beforehand or marked relevant) divided by the number of documents in the recall base for that request.

In the end, 303 requests were used for testing, with the results showing that the MEDLARS system was operating on average at about 58% recall and 50% precision. These averages cover a huge variation in performance across the requests. Figure 1.2 reproduces page 129 in the Lancaster report and shows a scatterplot of the results, broken down by the number of documents in the recall base. The results look almost random, due to the huge variation in performance across the requests. (The three curves show what Lancaster called the performance guarantees, i.e., what MEDLARS could guarantee their users: a 90% guarantee of performance for curve A, 80% for curve B, and 75% for curve C.)

The rest of his report contains detailed failure analysis for these requests. For each request Lancaster looked at the relevant documents that had been missed by the system (recall failures), and the documents that had been found by the system but judged non-relevant (the precision failures). This involved looking at the full text of each document, the indexing record for that document, user request statement, the manual search formulation, and the reasons the user had given for his judgments. This time-consuming examination led to detailed conclusions for each request, and his final chapter attempted to generalize based on these conclusions.

One generalization involved the performance levels, which were lower than expected. MED-LARS was retrieving an average of 175 citations per search at 58% recall and 50% precision. To operate at an average recall of 85-90% recall (and 20-25% precision), Lancaster estimated that 500 to 600 citations would have to be found and examined by the users. He polled a small sample of users and found that 5 out of those 8 users were happy with less than the maximum recall; his recommendation to MEDLARS was therefore to allow users to specify a high recall search rather than to try to boost their recall by always getting more citations.

The Lancaster study was a test of an operational system, with the goals of finding the problems in that one particular system. So whereas a test collection was built, and recall/precision was the metric for performance, the emphasis was on understanding the nature of the problems rather than experimenting with various parameters. His definition of relevance was more similar to utility, i.e., was this document of major or minor *value* to the user. Lancaster's method of measuring recall within a huge document base was unique; essentially a variation of today's known item retrieval methods. His careful selection of appropriate user groups, and getting "natural" requests from the users was critical to the study in terms of its results being accepted. And finally the methods of failure analysis, and the tremendous attention to detail in these analyses is a lesson for today's researchers.

## 1.4    THE SMART SYSTEM AND EARLY TEST COLLECTIONS

Gerard Salton started the SMART system at Harvard University in 1961, moving with it to Cornell University in 1965 [116, 146]. His initial interests were in the indexing structures used by manual indexers, but H.P. Luhn's suggestions [119] that simply using the words of a document for indexing might work was intriguing. The Harvard SMART framework was built to allow insertion of different

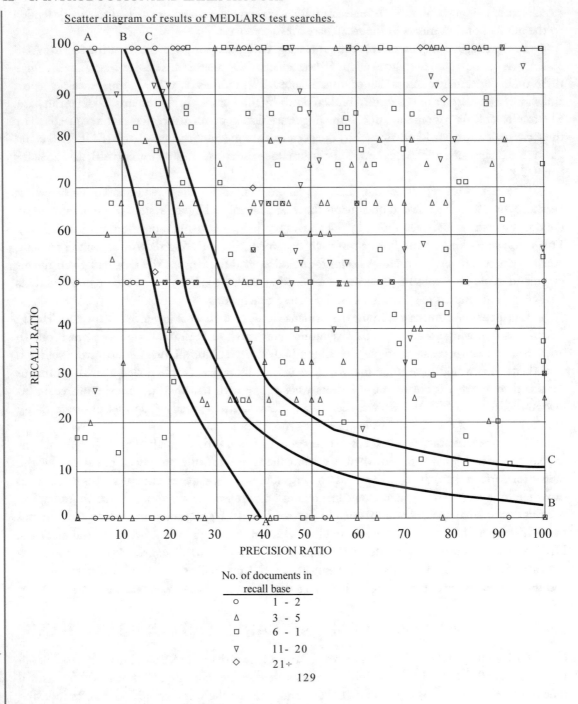

**Figure 1.2:** Scatter diagram of MEDLARS test searches.

software modules for experimentation with various indexing methods, such as citation indexing, thesaurus coding and the use of simple words. The SMART project continued at Cornell until Salton's death in 1995, producing enormous amounts of research that is documented in journals and proceedings and in the 22 "ISR"reports to NSF. A discussion of the research is beyond the scope of this lecture, but Salton's contributions to evaluation, especially in metrics and new test collections, are critical to the continuing saga of evaluation in information retrieval.

A major SMART evaluation contribution was in metrics, first started at Harvard by Joe Rocchio and continued at Cornell by Mike Keen (borrowed from the Cranfield project in 1966 and 1967). It should be remembered that the Cranfield and MEDLARS experiments were all working with single recall/precision points, e.g., each experiment in Cranfield or each request in Medlars generated a single recall/precision number. But the SMART experiments produced *ranked* or semi-ranked lists of documents, making it impossible to use the single-point recall/precision metrics. Salton and Rocchio proposed two sets of metrics called *rank recall* and *log precision* and *normalized recall* and *normalized precision* [102], both of which measured the differences between the actual ranked positions of the relevant documents and their "ideal" positions. Keen [107, 146] discussed and used the normalized ones for experiments, with the following definitions.

$$\text{Normalized recall} = 1 - \frac{\sum_{i=1}^{n} r_i - \sum_{i=1}^{n} i}{n(N - n)}$$

$$\text{Normalized precision} = 1 - \frac{\sum_{i=1}^{n} \log r_i - \sum_{i=1}^{n} \log i}{\log \frac{N!}{(N-n)!n!}}$$

$n$ = number of relevant documents,
$N$ = number of documents in collection,
$r_i$ = rank of $i$th relevant document,
$i$ = ideal rank position for the $i$th relevant item.

Keen also worked on further methodology for the recall/precision curves since he agreed with Cleverdon and Lancaster that it was important to provide separate recall and precision performances. The ranked results led naturally to recall/precision curves, but with problems as to where to make the actual measurements, i.e., the *cutoff points*. So for example one could plot the actual recall and precision for a set of queries at a fixed set of document cutoffs, e.g., 1,2,5,10,15 …documents retrieved; Keen called this the "Pseudo-Cranfield" method. The problem with this method is that queries had different numbers of relevant documents so these individual results did not average properly. Alternatively one could pick a fixed recall, e.g., 10%, 20%, … 100% and plot the precision at this point. However few queries have actual precision measurements at these exact recall points so interpolation was required, especially in the days of small collections (with small numbers of relevant documents). There were several types of interpolations proposed, including using the precision of the document with the highest precision at that recall point, the one with the lowest precision at that point, etc. The decision was to use the highest precision, the "Semi-Cranfield" method illustrated in the top graph in Figure 1.3. This figure (copied from Figure 17 in [107]) also shows the averages

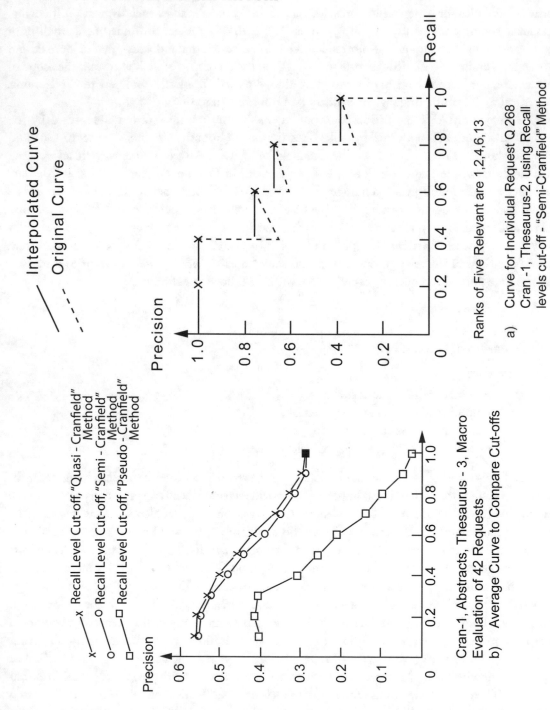

**Figure 1.3:** Illustrations of different methods of recall/precision interpolation

using three cutoff/interpolation methods in the bottom graph. It can be seen that the results from the document level method are very different from those using the recall-level methods. The final method that was used, called then the "Semi-Cranfield" method, is a variation of the quasi method that deals more appropriately with the frequent situation of two relevant documents adjacent in the ranking. This is the interpolated method used today, where the interpolated precision at a given recall-level is the maximum precision obtained at any recall point greater than or equal to that recall-level. Note that the performance differences for the various recall-level methods were slight even in those days of tiny collections.

There was continued discussion at Cornell in the mid 1960s about the micro vs. macro averaging issue (generally resolved in favor of using macro averaging now that a computer could do the calculations). Additionally there was work [39, 138, 139] with the generality measure (the percentage of documents in the collection that were relevant) since SMART had three versions of the Cranfield collection. There was the full collection of 1400 documents (Cran-1), the subcollection of 200 built by Cleverdon (Cran-2), and a second subcollection of 425 documents built at Cornell. A run on 1400 abstracts cost about $104 in 1965 (about $600 in today's dollar); very few runs were made on the full collection and therefore generality was an issue. As a final note on SMART's contribution to the metrics, it is important to realize that whereas there was discussion of these metrics with other IR researchers, and certainly some disagreements, once these were resolved, the field was able to move forward without many metrics "fights" and this has been a blessing for the whole IR field.

Another critical contribution was the idea of building a framework that allows for "easy" experimentation. The initial one at Harvard was updated to one at Cornell [146, 200] that allowed students to do one-semester projects with minimal recoding simply by changing of the parameter settings. This idea seems obvious today, but the framework and the availability of several test collections made information retrieval experimentation a routine process at a time when experimentation in most human language technology fields was still a difficult endeavor.

The final contribution of the SMART group to evaluation was a very large set of new test collections. All of these collections were built according to the Cranfield paradigm, with each collection designed and built using rigorous specifications. Usually these specifications were dictated by a specific goal for experimentation. Tables 1.2 and 1.3 lists the collections used by SMART, with all of these built in-house except those marked with an asterisk. The dates are approximate, based mostly on when they were first used in an experiment, and the various counts, etc. are taken from different sources so there will be small discrepancies. The number of queries shown is the number of queries with relevant documents, with the number of relevant being an average per query. The lengths of the documents and the queries are (mostly) after stopword removal and stemming, and any large inconsistencies are likely to come from counting unique terms vs. counting all terms, not removing stopwords, or using different stemmers (this was unfortunately seldom documented). What follows is a short description of how each collection was built, both for historical purposes and to illustrate various issues in test collection construction.

The first collection built was the IRE-1 collection of 405 abstracts from computer literature published in the 1959 IRE Transactions of Electronic Computers (and keypunched at Harvard). Salton was interested in how document analysis processes affected results, and had over 35 different document processing options in 1965. For example he used a "null thesaurus" consisting of automatically-created word stems, a manually-constructed thesaurus of 600 concepts in computer literature corresponding to 3000 word stems, hierarchical arrangements of those concepts, statistical phrases, syntactic analysis, etc. [108, 142, 145]. Note that these experiments were investigating similar themes to the Cranfield experiments, with the major exceptions being that these searches were carried out automatically once the document analysis was done, and that the returned results were ranked lists of documents, not single points per experiment. The 17 initial requests (queries) for the IRE-1 collection were built by three project staff, two of which had extensive knowledge of the system (but no knowledge of how it would actually perform). These three people also made the relevance assessments by looking at *all* the abstracts. The collection was extended using similar abstracts and 17 requests written by one non-staff person to become the IRE-3 collection.

The second early collection, the ADI collection, was a set of short papers from the 1963 Annual Meeting of the American Documentation Institute, keypunched at Harvard. The requests this time were created by two technical staff not familiar with the system, and once again these people made relevance judgments against the full collection. The reasons for building the ADI collection were similar to the earlier IRE one, but in addition there were titles, abstracts, and full texts, and this allowed experimentation with document lengths [106, 146]. Note that unlike the Cranfield collection, the first two SMART collections made no effort to get "real" user requests; however, Salton was careful to specify that the requests were not derived from the documents and therefore avoided the issue of the source documents that had caused Cleverdon so much pain [108].

The full Cranfield collection of abstracts was also keypunched at Harvard, allowing comparisons to Cleverdon's results, and the use of a very large collection compared to the two earlier ones. SMART mostly used the Cran-2 collection (200 documents), with stemmers and using the thesaurus previously built at Cranfield. As mentioned before, the cost of the runs allowed few runs with the full 1400 collection; eventually in 1969/1970 a "slimmed down" version of Cranfield with 424 documents and 155 queries was built by first eliminating the source documents, then the documents that were not relevant to any query, and finally creatively finding ways of reducing the documents to 424 while keeping as many queries as possible [116].

Having set up the basic experiments with these three collections, Salton moved on to tackle two thorny issues. The first issue was the continued strong criticisms of these evaluations based on the lack of realistic queries and on the unreliability of the relevance judgments. These issues had plagued the Cranfield experiments and a new test collection, the ISPRA collection, was built specifically to address this problem [117, 146]. The ISPRA documents were 1268 abstracts in the field of documentation and library science from American Documentation and several other journals (all again keypunched at Harvard). The queries this time were very carefully built by 8 library science students or professionals. Each person was asked to construct 6 requests that might actually be asked

Table 1.2:  SMART test collections

| Collection | Year | #Docs | #Questions | why built |
|---|---|---|---|---|
| Cran-2* | 1964 | 1398 | 225 | compare indexing methods |
| Cran-1* | 1964 | 200 | 42 | Cranfield subset of 42 questions |
| Cran424 | 1970 | 424 | 155 | Cornell "reduced" subset |
| IRE-3 | 1965 | 780 | 34 | indexing/dictionary experiments |
| ADI | 1965 | 82 | 35 | doc length experiments |
| ISPRA | 1967 | 1268 | 48 | multiple relevance judgements |
| ISPRA | 1968 | 1095/468 | 48 | CLIR English/German |
| MED273 | 1967 | 273 | 18 | comparison to Lancaster |
| MED450 | 1970 | 450 | 30 | "corrected" Medlars |
| MEDLARS | 1970 | 1033 | 30 | larger medical collection |
| OPHTH. | 1970 | 853 | 30 | specific medical domain |
| TIME | 1970 | 425 | 83 | full text articles |
| NPL* | 1970 | 11429 | 93 | indexing experiments |
| INSPEC* | 1982 | 12684 | 84 | indexing, Boolean |
| CACM | 1982 | 3204 | 52 | additional metadata |
| ISI/CISI | 1982 | 1460 | 76 | co-citations |

Table 1.3:  SMART test collections

| Collection | Doc.length | Quest.length | #relevant | comments |
|---|---|---|---|---|
| Cran-2* | 53.1 | 9.2 | 7.2 | #unique terms in abstract |
| Cran-1* | 91 | 8 | 4.7 | no source docs |
| Cran424 | 83.4 | 8 | 6.4 | fixed # of docs, no source docs |
| IRE-3 | 49 | 12 | 17.4 | |
| ADI | 710/35/7 | 8 | 4.9 | text, abstracts, title lengths |
| ISPRA | abstracts | longer | 17.8 | relevant by author |
| ISPRA | abstracts | longer | 14.2/13.6 | relevant English/German |
| MED273 | 60? | 9.3 | 4.8/11.1 | precision/recall bases |
| MED450 | 64.8 | 10.1 | 9.2 | |
| MEDLARS | 51.6 | 10.1 | 23.2 | |
| OPHTH. | 60? | 10? | 30 | |
| TIME | 263.8 | 16.0 | 8.7 | |
| NPL* | 20.0 | 7.2 | 22.4 | |
| INSPEC* | 32.5 | 15.6 | 33.0 | |
| CACM | 24.5 | 10.8 | 15.3 | |
| ISI/CISI | 46.5 | 28.3 | 49.8 | |

by library science students. There was a detailed set of instructions containing criteria such as "use from 50 to 100 words and up to 3 sentences", "do not submit queries corresponding to the contents of a specific document", "do not rephrase specific document contents", etc. The relevance criteria was also strict: an abstract was considered relevant only "if it is directly stated in the abstract as printed, or can be directly deduced from the printed abstract, that the document contains information on the topic asked for in the query". Relevance judgments were made by the original query author *and* by one of the other professionals. The average agreement between these two was found to be only 30%, however similar to later experiments in TREC, it was shown that the performance ranking of the various processing methods, such as words vs. stems and thesaurus vs. stems *did not change* depending on the relevance judgment set that was used [117, 146].

The ISPRA collection was also used to test cross-language retrieval [137, 146]. The English abstracts were 1095 taken from the initial ISPRA collection; additionally there were 468 German abstracts for the collection. The same 48 queries were used, with translations to German done by a native German speaker; the relevance assessments against the German abstracts were done by a different native German speaker.

Salton's second issue was the need to show that the SMART system, e.g., a ranking system using the naturally-occurring terms in the documents and queries, was equivalent to the manually-indexed Boolean retrieval systems [116]. Proving this required showing that the SMART system could scale to operational-size collections; this issue drove many of the clustering theses during those days. But it also caused the creation of the first Medlars collection [143, 146]. The collection was based on the Lancaster study, with 18 of the queries that had been used in that study, along with 273 of the 518 abstracts (the others were not in English or not easily available). The problem came in the comparison of the results. Lancaster had measured his recall and precision by using two *separate* collections: the recall base and the precision base. Additionally he had computed a single recall and precision for each query. The comparison of a ranked list to a single point was one problem, but this was compounded by many other problems and the final solutions (see [143, 146]) show both the creativity and the dedication to proper testing methods possessed by Salton and Keen.

A second Medlars collection was built in 1970 [140, 141] in order to do a better comparison. Twelve more of the original Lancaster requests were added to the original 18 queries, and documents that had been identified as relevant from all of the 30 requests were checked against the Science Citation Index to find a total of 15 additional citations (per request) that were in MEDLARS. These citations were added to the SMART collection and a medical student reviewed them for relevance. This student first tried 6 other MEDLARS requests and had a 69% agreement with the original users and this was felt to be sufficient based on the earlier ISPRA study. The third and final version of the Medlars collection was an expansion by adding a total of 583 relevant documents from the recall bases for the 30 queries.

Around the same time, an ophthalmology collection was built from "scratch" using 30 real user requests and the document set that was retrieved for these requests. The relevance assessments were (mostly) all done by a medical student. The goal of this second medical collection was to allow comparison between a "general" medical collection (the large Medlars one) and one in a specific domain.

The final test collection of this busy period was a long-planned collection from TIME magazine. Here the goal was to build a collection of longer documents that were not in a scientific domain. The 425 documents were taken from an old print tape [116] and converted to SMART format. The problem was finding a useful query set. After several different tries, 83 questions were taken from four different sources: the New York Times News of the Week news questions (44), the New York Times Current Affairs Test for Colleges (27), the TIME Current Affair Test (7) and Senior Scholastic columns (5). These questions all involved news issues in 1963 and were selected from a total of 182 questions from these sources. Once again, one person made all of the relevance judgments (all questions for all documents).

Two other collections from this period were imported. The NPL collection came from Britain and is discussed in the next section on the British collections. The INSPEC collection came from Syracuse University, where the topics had been built in several versions by information science students as part of a project; the documents were abstracts in electrical engineering from the INSPEC database.

This initial set of test collections was heavily used, particularly the Cranfield424, TIME, and MED450 set (for example, see [144]). There were no more collections built until a very energetic graduate student (Ed Fox) built two much more complex collections in 1982 [69]. These collections, the CACM and ISI ones, were constructed specifically to test the use of multiple concept types as input to the system, such as bibliographic citations/co-citations.

The CACM documents covered all articles in issues of the CACM from 1958 to 1979. The data contained the titles and abstracts for automatic indexing, but also the authors, the computing reviews categories, the citations, the co-citations, and the links (references to or citations between articles). This complex set of information was used in different types of Boolean queries for Fox's thesis. The queries for this collection were true user queries, gathered from faculty, staff and students from various U.S. computer science departments. The relevance judgments were performed by these users, but only on specially selected documents that were likely to be relevant (selected in a manner similar to the pooling operation done in TREC but using only various SMART runs).

The ISI collection was specifically selected because of the co-citation data involved. The 1460 documents were based on a set of information science documents published between 1969 and 1977 that had been collected by Dr. Henry Small. The abstracts, titles and author list were used, along with information allowing co-citation vectors to be produced. The queries were the same queries as the ADI collection (35) plus 41 queries from the ISPRA collection that had relevant documents in this collection and some more modern queries constructed from the abstracts section of the SIGIR Forum. Four members of the SMART project did exhaustive relevance judgments.

Most of these collections became the basis for information retrieval evaluation for over 20 years and illustrate the evolving science of test collection construction. First there was the insistence on realistic test quest ons, and then the fuller understanding of the effects of relevance judging that came from the ISPRA experiment, which showed that single non-user judges could be employed. The test collections are all excellent examples of the Cranfield paradigm, but in hindsight they exhibit unexpected problems (in addition to being very small). For example the Medlars collections have an extremely high ratio of relevant documents to non-relevant documents because of the particular construction of the document set. Additionally the queries have words that are very specific, making it easy to retrieve the relevant documents at a high rank and therefore "everything works on Medlars". Note that each of these collections were built correctly for their initial goals; the problem is that later experimenters used the collections for *different* goals and were unaware of these biases.

   Chris Buckley specifically looked at the 7 still existing collections in his series of weighting runs in the mid 1980s, and reached the following conclusions [116].

- CACM: Avoid document length normalization experiments (strong bias towards long relevant documents)

- NPL: Avoid idf experiments (Queries are short, and all terms are equally good)

- CRAN: Be careful of tf experiments. Title is simply first sentence, so all terms duplicated.

- MEDLARS: Avoid relevance feedback or expansion experiments (documents cluster around queries)

- TIME: Too small, but otherwise good.

- CISI: Poorness of results means random factors can dominate. Bimodal distribution of query lengths a problem.

- INSPEC: Relevance judgements are suspect, but otherwise OK

## 1.5   THE COMPARATIVE SYSTEMS LABORATORY AT CASE WESTERN UNIVERSITY

In about the same timeframe as the Medlars study and the SMART system, the Comparative Systems Laboratory (CSL) [152] was created by Tefko Saracevic at the Case Western University in Cleveland. This project was notable not only for further innovations in evaluation but also for a "parallel" course [151] linked to the laboratory that allowed students to share in the excitement of live research (similar to students working with the SMART system). The CSL work was done from 1963 to 1968, resulting in a massive report which was summarized in [152]. Saracevic was interested in testing various indexing and (manual) search variables, but additionally had the goal of gaining "a further understanding of the variables and processes operating within retrieval systems and of methodologies needed for experimentation with such systems". His test collection was built in a similar manner to the Cranfield 2 work, starting with a document collection of 600 full-text articles on tropical diseases (which represented about half of the open literature at that time), and questions gathered from 25 user volunteers from 13 organizations who were specialists in their field and who were asked to "provide questions related to their current research interest". The documents were then indexed (by trained indexers using a manual) with five different indexing languages: telegraphic abstract (index terms assigned without constraints including syntactic roles and links), keywords selected by indexers, keywords selected by a computer program, a metalanguage and the Tropical Disease Bulletin index terms. The indexing was done on titles and abstracts and full-text for the first three languages, resulting in 5 to 8 terms for titles, 23 to 30 terms for abstracts, and 36 to 40 terms for full-text.

There were 124 questions gathered from the users that were then used for searching with five types of question analysis done on each question (unit concepts (A), expansion of A using a thesaurus (B), expansion of A using other tools (C), further expansion of C using thesaurus (D), and E which was a user-verified version of D). Note that these question analysis types were mirroring the types of "natural" steps that a search intermediary might make, as opposed to the more constrained approach to searching that was used in Cranfield. However there was extensive checking of the searches for consistency with over half being re-run with errors fixed. Additionally all of the searches were done in both a narrow method based strictly on the question analysis and a broader search statement looking at a more general subject aspect.

The relevance judgments were created using a type of pooling method, i.e., a *universal set* was created by the union of all sets of outputs from all the indexing strategies the question analysis strategies and all searching strategies. These universal sets were then judged by the 25 users on a three-point scale: relevant ("any document which on the basis of the information it conveys, is considered to be related to your question even if the information is outdated or familiar"), partially-relevant ("any document which on the basis of the information it conveys is considered only somewhat or in some part related to your question or to any part of your question"), and nonrelevant. The judgments made were clearly stringent, with over half of the questions having no relevant documents, and 80% of the remaining questions having only one to five relevant.

The metrics used were *sensitivity* (defined the same as recall) and *specificity* which is the number of nonrelevant documents NOT retrieved divided by the total number of nonrelevant documents in the universal set. Both of these metrics were calculated over all queries, i.e., the micro-averaging method used in Cranfield, along with a combined metric *effectiveness* which was defined as sensitivity plus specificity minus one.

The paper [152] contains a thorough analysis of the indexing schemes, the question-analysis schemes, and the searching strategies, coming to many of the same conclusions as both Cleverdon and Lancaster. This project, however, was the first to employ real user questions and relevance judgments, and also the first to try pooling as a method of lowering the effort for relevance judging. An interesting note on the pooling is that only three of the five indexing schemes were operational in time for the initial pooling (retrieving a total of 1518 answers); however, when the other index files were added, there were 1108 additional answers almost all of which were nonrelevant. Saracevic noted that "this finding is taken to demonstrate that the files responded equally well in retrieving relevant answers, but that there were large, symmetric differences in the retrieval of non-relevant answers", something that is still seen today in batch evaluations.

## 1.6   CAMBRIDGE AND THE "IDEAL" TEST COLLECTION

In the mid 1960s Roger Needham (eventually joined by Karen Spärck Jones) was working on a theory of clumping of terms using automatic classification techniques [125]. This was applied to the Cranfield 200 collection with the goal of finding if these classifications were useful for information retrieval [165]. Whereas only the manually indexed version of the collection was used (rather than the actual words in the abstract and text), this work could be nicely compared with both Cleverdon's and Salton's results. However Spärck Jones was not satisfied with simply using the Cranfield collection, but went on to use two other collections, an INSPEC collection of 541 documents (different than the one used by SMART), and a new collection by Mike Keen, the ISILT collection [110]. Unfortunately the results were different for each collection [163] and this led to a serious interest in the properties of test collections.

It also led to a proposal in 1975 by Spärck Jones and Keith van Rijsbergen [166] for the creation of large test collection(s). The proposal had two overarching criteria: first, that it would allow for commonality of testing across retrieval researchers, and second that it would be adequate for many various projects. It should be noted that in 1975 the SMART collections (other than the Cranfield ones) were not only small in size, but lacked manual indexing and other "hooks" for document analysis. The group at Cambridge and other British researchers continued to be more interested in the document analysis part of information retrieval, such as finding better ways of indexing the documents, rather than the searching stage of retrieval.

This is why Spärck Jones had chosen to use the British collections for her work in 1973, and her proposal presented details of British collections as background material and as a basis for the new collection(s). Four of these are minimally described here to show the contrast in goals and construction with the SMART collections, and to motivate some of the issues in the proposal.

The ISILT collection was from Mike Keen, then at the University College of Wales in Aberwystwyth. There were 800 documents from the area of documentation, with 63 real requests and exhaustive relevance judgments by subject experts. The purpose of this collection was to continue to investigate manual indexing using five kinds of manual index terms. Three additional British collections also involved indexing studies. The INSPEC collection [4] used 542 documents in the sciences. The queries were based loosely on SDI profiles (Selective Dissemination of Information, where a library would select a limited set of citations to match an "SDI" profile), with the users asking a question that was within the scope of their SDI profile and then making relevance judgments only on those documents previously deemed relevant to their profile. Once again there were five types of manual indexing created. The UKCIS collection [19] was for Chemical Abstracts, testing the effectiveness of manually indexing titles, titles plus keywords, and titles plus digests. There were many digests/abstracts in several different subsets and 193 queries, again loosely based on SDI profiles and with user relevance judgments. Finally the NPL collection [181] had 11571 documents (which is why it was heavily used in the United States) from a published scientific abstract journal, with 93 requests based on source abstracts (similar to Cranfield). The documents were indexed semi-automatically using 1000 index terms and the purpose of the collection was to look at association between word pairs and clustering.

Note that all of these collections (with the exception of ISILT) used data from commercial search services. By using this type of data, the collections were guaranteed real user requests and also several types of manual indexing. This fitted in well with the kinds of experiments done in Cambridge, but also may have simply been what was available. The SMART collections were mainly built for the testing of the searching stage of retrieval and were funded by NSF. This allowed more freedom in creating collections, but also mostly negated the use of commercial search services.

Given this background, the proposal for the "ideal" test collection continued primarily in the British tradition of building test collections. The proposal was presented at a workshop and a six-month project at Cambridge worked on further details [164]. The following outline specification for the collection is quoted directly from this report.

1) Documents

Size: a main set of 30,000 documents broadly representative of service data bases in size and subject composition.

One or more other sets of 3000 documents complementing the main set in subject, etc. Thus, for example, if the main set was in a scientific area, one other set would in social science.

These sets would cover short time periods and English language material; they would have core characterizations. A random subset of the main set, containing 3000 documents, would be established, with enriched characterizations.

Properties: the main set, and the complementary other sets, would be heterogeneous on identified collection variables such as subject solidity, document type, author type, etc.

The size of the main set should permit the identification of subsets, say containing 3000 documents, which would be homogeneous on such variables.

In addition, one or more other sets would be required for time and language contrasts, and possibly for gross contrasts on other variables, for example covering monographs as opposed to articles. These would have core or enriched characterizations as appropriate or available.

2) Requests

Size: a primary set of 700-1000 requests would accompany the main set of documents.

Secondary sets of 150-250 requests would accompany other sets of documents.

As the primary sets would be of one form, envisaged as retrospective off-line queries, alternative sets representing different forms, e.g., SDI is one such method, and containing

150-250 requests were proposed for the main set. (At least some overlap of the primary and alternative sets through derivation from common need statements was suggested; this overlap would define a base set of 30 requests). These sets would have core characterizations. A random subset of the primary set, containing 150-250 requests, would be established, with enriched characterizations.

For document sets representing time and language contrasts, subsets of the primary set would be appropriate as requests.

Properties: the primary and alternative sets would be heterogeneous on such variables as topic type, user type, etc.

The size of the primary set should permit the selection of homogeneous subsets of perhaps 150 requests.

The request sets should represent many users, as well as many requests.

3) Relevance judgments

The proposals are not fully worked out and are further developed in (this) report. For reference, the main points were: default judgments by the users of their own search output; exhaustive judgments of the random subset of documents; pooled judgments on variant strategy search output; these would all use abstracts; checking judgments for the base set of requests, e.g., against the texts of the random subset, against another random subset, etc.

The data characterizations are:

a) core: for documents, all regular bibliographic information, abstracts, citations, natural language indexing, controlled language indexing, (using thesaurus terms or subject headings) and high level subject class codes, and an about sentence;

for requests, a verbal need statement, lists of free and controlled terms, and a Boolean specification.

b) enriched: for documents, a more exhaustive indexing, indexing from different sources, indexing by different people, PRECIS, etc; for requests, term weights, indexing by different people, etc.

Note that the variants for pooled judgments would constitute further request formulations.

Queries in the form of source documents should also be obtained.

It was proposed the full "sociological" background information relative to requests should be obtained.

c) relevance judgments; essential information would consist of two relevance grades and also a novelty indication; known relevant documents would be recorded. Judgments by different people would be covered by the basic design.

Appendix 7 of the report provided a theoretical basis for the construction of the relevance judgments. The approach was to create a "pool" of likely relevant documents and then obtain a limited number of relevance judgments for that pool (either by users or non-users). The pool was to be constructed by using different strategies (probably different document and request analysis strategies rather than searching strategies); then the total number of required assessments (number of requests multiplied by number of assessments per request) was to be estimated based on the requirement for significant differences between two potential strategies. A statistician was funded to further investigate this methodology, and a third report [74] provided detailed analysis of the proposed method and other possible methods. Further discussion of this report is beyond the scope of this lecture, but interested readers are strongly encouraged to invest some time here since the pooling issues are still difficult in today's testing methodology.

The 1977 report included information on possible document collections (very few machine-readable databases were available at that time), sources for requests (usually from commercial search services), and how the collections might be managed. This included cost estimates and also results of a survey on British groups that might use this collection. The final sentence of the report is as follows: "Thus if the BLR&DD can satisfy itself that, say 7 good projects will be forthcoming, "ideal" collection version D at £85K or even £100K is a good buy".

The "ideal" collection specifications have been provided here in such detail because it was not funded. The CACM collection built at Cornell had some of these characteristics, and a version of pooling was used in the relevance assessment, but it was not large, and it was built more for combining different search strategies than for document analysis. The large test collections that were dreamed of in 1975 were not built until 1992, and the TREC collections were not built based on these specifications but on other requirements (which are detailed in the next chapter).

A final result of the Cambridge investigation was a book "Information Retrieval Experiment" by Spärck Jones [167]. Published in 1981, it became a major influence in information retrieval evaluation, presenting chapters discussing different aspects of evaluation by most of the leading researchers at that time.

## 1.7    ADDITIONAL WORK IN METRICS UP TO 1992

The metrics used by Cleverdon and further developed by Salton and Keen for SMART were generally heavily used by all researchers. Several problems existed with these measures; most importantly that there was no easily-interpretable single measure of performance. By the late 1960s the normalized recall and precision had been replaced by several methods of averaging the recall-level values, such as averaging across 3 recall-levels, or 10 recall-levels, or 11 (including the two end points). But two other metrics were developed that have had significant use in the research community.

The first of these was William Cooper's expected search length [55]. His paper argued that not only was there no single measure, but that the various averages did not take into account how many relevant documents the user *actually* wanted. So his idea of the expected search length was to measure the "cost" to the user to find their desired number of relevant documents, which in the case of a ranked list is the number of *non-relevant* documents that they need to examine in order to satisfy their needs. The expected search length measure has often been used for the cases when only one relevant document, or a single "correct" document is the object of the search (known item searching).

The second metric to combine recall and precision was van Rijsbergen's E measure [180]. The E measure was defined for set-based retrieval, such as the Cranfield or Lancaster experiments, but could be extended to ranked list retrieval by calculating recall and precision at document cutoff levels, such as recall and precision at 20 documents.

$$E = 1 - \frac{1}{\alpha \frac{1}{P} + (1 - \alpha)\frac{1}{R}}$$

where $\alpha$ is a variable to control how much emphasis to put on precision versus recall, and $P$ and $R$ are the precision and recall values for the set being examined. Again this measure allows user requirements to be a part of the test by the use of the $\alpha$ parameter. However it works best for set retrieval rather than ranked list retrieval since use of the document level cutoff creates problems with averaging across sets of requests. A similar measure called the F measure (1 - E) is heavily used in classification experiments and natural language experiments where set retrieval is the norm.

The van Rijsbergen book [180]and the papers by Robertson [133] and Sanderson [147] are excellent reviews of the metrics in this period and are strongly recommended reading for both derivations of the metrics and comparisons across the various metrics that were proposed (including many not discussed here). Additionally the various chapters in the Spärck Jones book [167] discuss metrics, including ones by van Rijsbergen and Cooper.

CHAPTER 2

# "Batch" Evaluation Since 1992

## 2.1 INTRODUCTION

In 1992 a new large test collection became available to the information retrieval community. The TREC (Text REtrieval Evaluation Conference) collection and its sister evaluation efforts built on the Cranfield methods, extending the methodology where appropriate. This chapter elaborates on how these new test collections were created, how the various evaluations were designed, and what changes to the Cranfield methods had to be made. The later sections of the chapter summarize TREC's sister evaluations and discuss general lessons that can be drawn from all these evaluations.

## 2.2 THE TREC EVALUATIONS

The National Institutes of Standards (NIST) was asked in 1991 to build a test collection to evaluate the results of the DARPA (Defense Advanced Research Projects Agency) TIPSTER project [121] . The goal of this project was to significantly improve retrieval from large, real-world data collections, and whereas only four DARPA contractors were involved, the TREC initiative opened the evaluation to the wider information retrieval research community, with 25 additional groups taking part in 1992. TREC has now been running for nearly 20 years. Full coverage of the research is clearly beyond the scope of this lecture and readers are referred to [184] as a general reference and to the full series of online proceedings at http://trec.nist.gov/ for details relating to each year. However the details of the test collection methodology and the metrics presented in this chapter show the further evolution of evaluation for information retrieval

## 2.3 THE TREC AD HOC TESTS (1992-1999)

The term "ad hoc" here refers to the classic information retrieval user model used in the Cranfield method where ad hoc requests are searched against a fixed document collection. This section discusses the TREC ad hoc test methodology (test collection and metrics) in detail both because this methodology was extended for later TREC tasks (and other evaluation efforts) and because the ad hoc test collections are still heavily used in research today and it is important to understand how and why they were built.

### 2.3.1 BUILDING THE AD HOC COLLECTIONS

The TIPSTER/TREC test design was based squarely on the Cranfield paradigm, with a test collection of documents, user requests (called topics in TREC), and relevance judgments. Like Cranfield, it was important to create all parts of the collection based on a realistic user model, in this case the TIPSTER application. The TIPSTER users were presumed to be intelligence analysts, but could also be other types of users that work with information intensively, such as journalists, medical researchers, or legal staff.

The document collection needed to have a very large number of full-text documents (2 gigabytes of text was generally used each year), which needed to cover different timeframes and subject areas. They also had to be of varied length, writing style, level of editing and vocabulary. Table 2.1 lists the document sources used during the initial eight years of the ad hoc evaluations; these were selected based on availability and suitability to the TIPSTER task. Articles from newspapers and newswires covered all domains and contrasted in their format, style, and level of editing. Documents from *Computer Selects* were from different initial sources, but dealt with the single domain of computer technology. Finally there were documents selected less for their content than for the length of articles: the *Federal Register* ones were especially long, and of non-uniform length, and the DOE abstracts were very short. All documents were converted to a SGML-like format with enough uniformity to allow easy processing by the systems. Note that at 2 gigabtyes these collections were beyond the ability of most research systems in 1992 to handle, mainly because the storage to index them (say a total of 4 gigabytes) cost around $10,000 at that time.

Earlier test collections had typically provided only sentence-length requests; however, the TIPSTER/TREC topics contained multiple fields, including a user need statement that is a clear statement of what criteria make a document relevant. Having these multiple fields allowed for a wide range of query construction methods, and having clear statements about relevancy improved the consistency of relevance judgments. All topics were designed to mimic a real user's need, although the actual topic writers, the topic format and the method of construction evolved over time. The first two TRECs (topics 1-150) involved actual users of a TIPSTER-like search system and had very elaborate topics. By TREC-3 the topics were reduced to three fields and were written by the same group of "stand-in" users who did the relevance assessments. Figure 2.1 shows a sample topic from TREC-3. Each topic contains a number and title, followed by a one-sentence description of the information need. The final section is the narrative section, meant to be a full description of the information need in terms of what separates a relevant document from a nonrelevant document.

The definition of relevance has always been problematic in building information retrieval test collections [26, 36, 56, 85, 103]. The TIPSTER task was defined to be a high-recall task where it was important not to miss information. Therefore the assessors were instructed to judge a document relevant if information from that document would be used in some manner for the writing of a report on the subject of the topic, even if it was just one relevant sentence or if that information had already been seen in another document. This also implies the use of binary relevance judgments; that is, a document either contains useful information and is therefore relevant, or it does not. Documents retrieved for each topic were judged by a single assessor so that all documents screened would reflect the same user's interpretation of topic.

**Table 2.1:** Document collection statistics.

|  | Size: MB | # Docs | Median # Words | Mean # Words |
|---|---|---|---|---|
| **Disk 1** | | | | |
| *Wall Street Journal* | | | | |
| 1987–1989 | 267 | 98,732 | 245 | 434.0 |
| *Associated Press* 1989 | 254 | 84,678 | 446 | 473.9 |
| *Computer Selects* | 242 | 75,180 | 200 | 473.0 |
| *Federal Register* 1989 | 260 | 25,960 | 391 | 1315.9 |
| abstracts from DOE | 184 | 226,087 | 111 | 120.4 |
| **Disk 2** | | | | |
| *Wall Street Journal* | | | | |
| 1990–1992 | 242 | 74,520 | 301 | 508.4 |
| *Associated Press* 1988 | 237 | 79,919 | 438 | 468.7 |
| *Computer Selects* | 175 | 56,920 | 182 | 451.9 |
| *Federal Register* 1988 | 209 | 19,860 | 396 | 1378.1 |
| **Disk 3** | | | | |
| *San Jose Mercury News* 1991 | 287 | 90,257 | 379 | 453.0 |
| *Associated Press* 1990 | 237 | 78,321 | 451 | 478.4 |
| *Computer Selects* | 345 | 161,021 | 122 | 295.4 |
| U.S. patents, 1993 | 243 | 6,711 | 4445 | 5391.0 |
| **Disk 4** | | | | |
| *Financial Times* | | | | |
| 1991–1994 | 564 | 210,158 | 316 | 412.7 |
| *Federal Register* 1994 | 395 | 55,630 | 588 | 644.7 |
| *Congressional Record* 1993 | 235 | 27,922 | 288 | 1373.5 |
| **Disk 5** | | | | |
| Foreign Broadcast Information | | | | |
| Service | 470 | 130,471 | 322 | 543.6 |
| *Los Angeles Times* | | | | |
| 1989-1990 | 475 | 131,896 | 351 | 526.5 |

There was the additional requirement that the relevance assessments be as complete as possible. This became a critical piece of both the implementation of TREC and the later analysis of the collections. Three possible methods for finding the relevant documents could have been used. In the first method, full relevance judgments could have been made on over a million documents for each topic, resulting in over 100 million judgments (clearly impossible). The second approach, a true non-

```
<num> Number: 168
<title> Topic: Financing AMTRAK

<desc> Description:
A document will address the role of the Federal Government in
financing the operation of the National Railroad Transportation
Corporation (AMTRAK).

<narr> Narrative:
A relevant document must provide information on the government's
responsibility to make AMTRAK an economically viable entity. It
could also discuss the privatization of AMTRAK as an alternative
to continuing government subsidies. Documents comparing
government subsidies given to air and bus transportation with
those provided to AMTRAK would also be relevant.
```

**Figure 2.1:** Sample topic statement from TREC-3

biased random sample of the documents, would have been prohibitively expensive for acceptable completeness levels. Therefore a biased sampling method called "pooling" was adopted from the 1977 proposal to the British Library for building an "ideal" test collection [164]. To construct the pools for TREC, the following was done. Given a ranked list of results from a single system, for each topic select the top X ranked documents for input to the pool. Then merge this set with sets from all systems, sort the final list based on the document identifiers, and remove duplicates (identical documents found by multiple systems in the pool). This created the pooled list for each topic that was then judged by the assessors.

## 2.3.2    ANALYSIS OF THE AD HOC COLLECTIONS

Since the ad hoc evaluations were run for 8 years (see Table 2.2 for details of the eight collections), it was possible to analyze how well the various evaluation decisions were working and to modify them as necessary. This analysis is presented in detail here because these large collections are still in heavy use and it is critical to know their strengths and weaknesses in order to avoid experimental bias. It also provides guidance for some of the types of issues that need to be investigated in building future test collections.

The document selection and semi-standardized formatting worked very well. Groups had little trouble indexing the documents (other than scaling issues), and had no problems with domain or time elements. Analysis showed that by far the largest number of relevant documents came from the document sources covering all domains: *Wall Street Journal* (WSJ) and *Associated Press* (AP). In

Table 2.2: Document and topics sets for the first 8 TRECs.

| TREC ad hoc | Document sets | Topic Numbers |
|---|---|---|
| TREC-1 | disks 1 & 2 | 51-100 |
| TREC-2 | disks 1 &2 | 101-150 |
| TREC-3 | disks 1 & 2 | 151-200 |
| TREC-4 | disks 2 &3 | 201-250 |
| TREC-5 | disks 2 & 4 | 251-300 |
| TREC-6 | disks 4 &5 | 301-350 |
| TREC-7 | disks 4 & 5 (minus Congressional Record) | 351-400 |
| TREC-8 | disks 4 &5 (minus Congressional Record) | 401-450 |

contrast, the very long *Federal Register* (FR) documents had few relevant documents, but in TREC-2 most retrieval systems had difficulty in screening out these long documents. By TREC-3 this effect had disappeared as most of the systems made major corrections in their term weighting algorithms between TRECs 2 and 3 and thus could cope with any length document.

The ad hoc topics built for TREC underwent major evolution across the first five TRECs. Part of this evolution came as a result of changes in the personnel constructing the topics, but most was the result of deliberate changing of the topic specifications. The elaborate topics in the first two TRECs contained a field with manually-selected keywords (the concepts field) and this was removed in TREC-3 because it was felt that real user questions would not contain this field, and because inclusion of the field discouraged research into techniques for expansion of "too short" user need expressions. The TREC-4 topics were made even shorter, with removal of the title and the narrative field, however this turned out to be too short, especially for groups building manual queries, so the TREC-3 format became standard.

There was also a change in how the topics were constructed. In TREC-3 the assessors brought in "seeds" of topics, i.e., ideas of issues on which to build a topic. These seeds were then expanded by the assessor, based on looking at the items that were retrieved. To avoid this tuning to the data, starting in TREC-4 the assessors were asked to bring in a one-sentence description that was used for the initial searching to estimate the number of relevant documents that are likely to be found. Topics with "reasonable" numbers of relevant documents were then kept for further development into the final TREC ad hoc topics.

Another issue about the topics relates to measuring the difficulty of a given topic. There has been no attempt in TREC to build topics to match any particular characteristics, partly because the emphasis was on real user topics, but also because it is not clear what particular characteristics would be appropriate. A measure called topic "hardness" was defined for each topic as the average over a given set of runs of the precision at R (where R is the number of relevant documents for that topic) *OR* the precision at 100 if there were more than 100 relevant documents. This measure is therefore oriented towards high recall performance and how well systems do at finding all the relevant documents. In TREC-5 an attempt was made to correlate topic characteristics with this hardness measure, but neither topic length nor the number of relevant documents were found to be correlated [191], and it is still unclear what topic characteristics make a topic harder. Further work on topic characteristics has been carried out in an extended workshop, the Reliable Information Access (RIA) workshop in 2004 [82].

A related issue concerns the "required" number of topics for a test collection, i.e., how many topics are needed in order for the performance averages to be stable, much less show significant differences between systems or techniques. There has always been a huge variability in the performance across topics, as seen in the Lancaster experiments described earlier or in the selection of the large number (221) of requests in the Cranfield collection. TREC was no exception here, with a huge variability in the "hardness" of the topics, in the system performance on each topic, and in the performance of different techniques, such as relevance feedback on each topic. However it is critical that the average performance measure truly reflect differences rather than just random performance points. It was "folklore", at least in the SMART project, that a minimum of 25 topics were needed. Although TREC's 50 topic sets have been shown to produce stable averages [34, 189], the measurement of significant differences is still a problem in information retrieval, with some TREC-specific work starting in TREC-3 [173], and much more work since then (see Chapter 5 in [147]).

The TREC relevance judgments were specifically designed to model users interested in high recall tasks and therefore the more complete the relevance judgments are, the better the test collection models the high-recall needs of these users. Additionally, the more complete the test collection, the more likely that future systems using the collection for evaluation can trust that all/most of the relevant documents in the collection have been identified. Note that the pooling methodology *assumes* that all documents that have not been judged can be considered non-relevant.

A test of the relevance judgment completeness assumption was made using TREC-2 results, and again during the TREC-3 evaluation. In both cases, a second set of 100 documents was examined from each system, using only a sample of topics and systems in TREC-2, and using all topics and systems in TREC-3 [78, 79]. The more complete TREC-3 testing found well less than one new relevant document per run. These levels of completeness are quite acceptable; furthermore the number of new relevant documents found was shown to be more strongly correlated with the original number of relevant documents, i.e., topics with many relevant documents are more likely to have additional ones, than with the number of documents judged.

These findings were independently verified by Justin Zobel at the Royal Melbourne Institute of Technology (RMIT) [204]. Additionally Zobel found that lack of completeness did not bias the results of particular systems and that systems that did not contribute documents to the pool can still be evaluated fairly using the pooled judgments. Since the goal of the TREC collections is to allow comparisons of multiple runs, either across systems or within systems, having the exact number of relevant documents, or having an exact recall number is not as important as knowing that the judgments are complete enough to insure that comparisons of two methods using the test collections will be accurate.

A second issue important to any set of relevance judgments is their consistency, i.e., how stable are the judgments and how does their stability or lack thereof affect comparison of performance of systems using that test collection. Salton investigated this during the ISPRA experiments [117, 146] and Cleverdon also did a small experiment [50] showing minimal effects on system comparison. For TREC each topic was judged by a single assessor to ensure the best consistency of judgment and testing of this consistency was done after TREC-2, and more completely for TREC-4 [78, 80]. All the ad hoc topics had samples rejudged by two additional assessors, with the results being about 72% agreement (using the overlap measure of the intersection over the union) among all three judges, and 88% agreement between the initial judge and either one of the two additional judges. This remarkably high level of agreement is probably due to the similar background and training of the judges, and a general lack of ambiguity in the topics as represented by the narrative section.

Unfortunately, most of this agreement was for the large numbers of documents that were clearly nonrelevant. Whereas less than 3% of the initial nonrelevant documents were marked as relevant by secondary judges, 30% of the documents judged relevant by the initial judge were marked as nonrelevant by both the additional judges. This average hides a high variability across topics; for 12 of the 50 topics the disagreement on relevant documents was higher than 50%.

While some of these disagreements were likely caused by mistakes, most of them were caused by human variation in judgment, often magnified by a mismatch between the topic statement, the task, and the document collection. For example, topic 234 is "What progress has been made in fuel cell technology?". A lenient interpretation might declare relevant most documents that discuss fuel cells. A strict judge could require that relevant documents literally present a progress report on fuel cell technology. Additionally some of the more problematic topics were either very open to different interpretations (topic 245: "What are the trends and developments in retirement communities?") or so badly mismatched to the document collection that the initial assessor made extremely lenient relevance judgments (topic 249: "How has the depletion or destruction of the rain forest effected the worlds weather?").

Note this topic and user variation is very realistic and must be accepted as part of any testing. Users come to retrieval systems with different expectations, and most of these expectations are unstated. If test collections do not reflect this noisy situation, then the systems that are built using these collections to test their algorithms will not work well in operational settings.

A critical question is how all this variation affects system comparisons. Voorhees [185] investigated this by using different subsets of the relevance judgments from TREC-4. As her most stringent test, she used the intersection of the relevant document sets (where all judges had agreed), and the union of these judgements (where any judge had marked a document relevant). She found that although the mean average precision of a given set of system results did change, the changes were highly correlated across systems and the relative ranking of different system runs did not significantly change. Even when the two runs were from the same organization (and therefore are more likely to be similar), the two systems were ranked in the same order by all subsets of relevance judgments. This clearly demonstrates the stability of the TREC ad hoc relevance judgments in the sense that groups can test two different algorithms and be reasonably assured that results reflect a true difference between those algorithms.

These results were independently verified as a result of the University of Waterloo's work in TREC-6 [57]. Waterloo personnel judged over 13,000 documents for relevance, and these judgments were used by Voorhees in a similar manner as the TREC-4 multiple judgments. Even though there was even less agreement between the NIST assessors and the Waterloo assessors (very different backgrounds and training), the changes in system rankings were still not significant. The one exception to this was the comparison between two same-system runs in which one run had used manual relevance feedback. For this reason, comparison between automatic runs and runs with manual intervention, particularly manual relevance feedback which basically adds a third relevance judge, should be more carefully analyzed as they are the comparisons most likely to be affected by variations in relevance judgments.

### 2.3.3    THE TREC AD HOC METRICS

TREC followed the Cranfield metrics, essentially using the metrics developed by Mike Keen and Gerard Salton discussed earlier. Starting in TREC-1 Chris Buckley made available the evaluation program used by SMART called trec_eval. Researchers in the field at this time were using various metrics from SMART, but with different implementations and with different choices of which metrics to report. This made comparison across systems difficult and the availability of a standard package at least made for a common implementation of these metrics.

Figure 2.2 shows the set of metrics provided for a run in the TREC-8 ad hoc track. The recall level and document level precision averages across the 50 topics are shown, in addition to a new non-interpolated average precision, defined as "the precision at each relevant document, averaged over all relevant documents for a topic" [33]. The non-interpolated average precision is then averaged over all the topics to produce the "mean average precision" or MAP, which has been used as the main measure in TREC. Other new metrics include the R-Precision which was proposed by Buckley to better measure the high-recall task being modeled in TREC. For more details on these metrics, including a discussion of their relative strengths and weaknesses, see [33, 147]. Note that this result page also includes a histogram showing the results for all of the 50 topics so that groups could easily spot how their systems had performed with respect to the median system performance per topic.

## 2.4    OTHER TREC RETRIEVAL TASKS

New tasks called tracks were added in TREC-4, and led to the design and building of many specialized test collections. None of these test collections were as extensive as nor as heavily used as the ad hoc collections described earlier, but the necessary changes in the design criteria provide useful case studies in building test collections. Note that these changes were required either because of the specific data characteristics, or because the track research goals dictated modifications to the standard Cranfield implementation. The track descriptions that follow are ordered by the amount

Ad hoc results — SabIR Research/Cornell University

| Summary Statistics | |
| --- | --- |
| Run Number | Sab8A4 |
| Run Description | Automatic, title + desc |
| Number of Topics | 50 |
| Total number of documents over all topics | |
| Retrieved: | 50000 |
| Relevant: | 4728 |
| Rel-ret: | 2986 |

| Recall Level Precision Averages | |
| --- | --- |
| Recall | Precision |
| 0.00 | 0.7860 |
| 0.10 | 0.5229 |
| 0.20 | 0.4324 |
| 0.30 | 0.3644 |
| 0.40 | 0.3084 |
| 0.50 | 0.2498 |
| 0.60 | 0.1912 |
| 0.70 | 0.1360 |
| 0.80 | 0.0776 |
| 0.90 | 0.0362 |
| 1.00 | 0.0133 |
| Average precision over all relevant docs non-interpolated | 0.2608 |

| Document Level Averages | |
| --- | --- |
| | Precision |
| At 5 docs | 0.5200 |
| At 10 docs | 0.4800 |
| At 15 docs | 0.4413 |
| At 20 docs | 0.4090 |
| At 30 docs | 0.3733 |
| At 100 docs | 0.2384 |
| At 200 docs | 0.1702 |
| At 500 docs | 0.0985 |
| At 1000 docs | 0.0597 |
| R-Precision (precision after R docs retrieved (where R is the number of relevant documents)) | |
| Exact | 0.3021 |

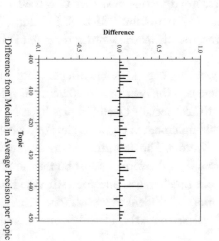

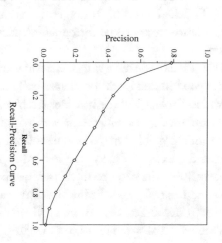

Figure 2.2: Sample evaluation report from TREC-8

of change that was necessary to the TREC ad hoc design, but in all cases there was a user model to guide the task definition (and hence the test collection), and to define the correct metrics.

## 2.4.1   RETRIEVAL FROM "NOISY" TEXT

Here the user model is still the ad hoc task, but the documents are "noisy" text, such as that produced by OCR scans or speech transcription, and the goal is to understand how retrieval performance is affected by this noise. In TREC-4 the ad hoc topics were used against artificially degraded *Wall Street Journal* data that reflected error rates of 10 and 20% character errors. For TREC-5 [191], a more sophisticated test used actual OCR data from the 1994 *Federal Register*, with comparison of results using the correct copy (electronic version), plus two scanned copies at 5% error rates and 20% error rates. The topics were changed to known item topics, i.e., each topic was created to uniquely retrieve one document, a type of search that is particularly useful for testing in "noisy" data, where a single corrupted term might cause a system to miss that document. The metric used to measure performance for this task was a variation of Cooper's expected search length [55], and was based on the rank where the item was retrieved. In this case however a measure called *mean-reciprocal-rank, MRR* was used to allow proper averaging. MRR is the mean of the reciprocal of the rank where the known item was found, averaged across all the topics, and is mathematically equivalent to the mean average precision when there is only one target document [183].

A second type of noisy text comes from speech recognition systems. Two groups at NIST, the Speech group and the Retrieval group, collaborated to implement test collections for broadcast news for TRECs 6-8 [73]. Note that for speech processing there is no clear definition of a document; documents were defined to be specific stories, usually separated by a change in speaker and/or a change in topic. Additionally the "documents" were provided both as text transcriptions of the data (manually or automatically transcribed) or as recorded waveforms. TREC-6 used a 50 hour set of news; TREC-7 used 87 hours, and there were 557 hours for TREC-8. In addition to the normal information retrieval performance metrics, the speech metric word error rate (WER) was also reported.

In 2001 TREC started a video retrieval track, working with 11 hours of video, and 74 known item searches contributed by the participants. This increased the next year to 40 hours of video from the Open Video Project and the Internet Archive, with 25 specially created topics from NIST. The topics were expressed in a multi-media way, with text supplemented by video clips or bits of speech in order to mimic possible types of requests from likely users. The definition of documents became more fuzzy as the extent of the video needed to respond to the topic had to be measured at shot boundaries. By 2003, the video retrieval task had become much more concerned with the image part of the video and the task was split into its own evaluation, TRECvid (http://www-nlpir.nist.gov/projects/trecvid/). For more on video retrieval, see both the TRECvid site and references from the video retrieval community such as [160].

## 2.4.2    RETRIEVAL OF NON-ENGLISH DOCUMENTS

TREC-3 began work with Spanish and Chinese to investigate how the retrieval techniques would work outside of English. The user model was still the ad hoc model, but with Spanish and Chinese topics and documents respectively. The only change necessary to the ad hoc model was the issue of character sets, including how to deal with the accents in Spanish and the Chinese character sets. One of the important lessons learned in this first evaluation was the importance of using native speakers in both topic generation and relevance judgments to reflect a real user model and to allow speedy relevance judgments!

But what if the user is trying to retrieve documents in a language that is not their native language? The user modeled for cross-language retrieval (CLIR) would be creating topics in their native language, which would then be searched across the set of other languages, since it is assumed that they have more proficiency in reading another language than in creating topics in that language. This implies that it is critical that the topics be created by native speakers in each language to insure that they reflect how a person would actually express their information need in that language.

The major impetus for the first CLIR track (TREC-6) was the creation of a document collection [156] that had "parallel" documents in three languages (French, German, and Italian) from the Swiss newswire *Schweizerische Depeschen Agentur*. English documents from the *AP* newswire in the same year were added, and all documents were put in the SGML-like format with a new field added to indicate the (major) language of that document. The 25 topics used the first year were written in three languages at NIST, however by the second year this became a co-operative effort across groups in Switzerland, Germany and Italy, with 56 topics written in four languages (English, French, German, and Italian) for TRECs 7 and 8 [29].

In order to balance input from the initial topic languages, equal numbers of topics were chosen from each site for the final topic set. The full set of topics were then translated to all four languages. Relevance judgments were made at all four sites for all topics, with each site examining only the pool of documents in their native language. This distributed scenario for building topics and making relevance judgments was a necessary but major departure from the Cranfield model.

Note that the effect of the distributed method of relevance judgments on results is probably small since the major distribution was across languages, not topics. As long as results are compared within the same language, i.e., pairs of results on German documents, and not across languages, i.e., results on English documents vs. German documents, there are no problems. However comparing results across different languages is both comparing across completely different document collections and across two human relevance judges and is not valid.

The European CLIR track moved to Europe after TREC-8 to become a separate evaluation (CLEF: http://www.clef-campaign.org/) and information about further work in CLEF is in a later section. TREC continued CLIR for three more years, first with English and Chinese, and finally for two years using English and Arabic.

### 2.4.3   VERY LARGE CORPUS, WEB RETRIEVAL, AND ENTERPRISE SEARCHING

Another issue in retrieval is the effect of much larger collections of documents, both on the retrieval results and on efficiency. David Hawking and his colleagues at CSIRO put together five large collections to test efficiency and later to test web applications [87]. This was piloted in TREC-6 with 20 gigabtyes of assorted text (called VLC1), but scaled up to 100 gigabytes of web data from the Internet archive (VLC2) the next year [86, 88]. The TREC-7 ad hoc topics were used against VLC2, but with very shallow pools (20 documents deep vs. 100), and whereas this test collection would not meet a completeness test, it was appropriate for normal high-precision web testing. In TREC-8, the "large" web track used the VLC2 data for 10,000 web queries from a search log (only a random sample of 50 were judged). Additionally the VLC2 data was appropriately down-sampled to create a "small" web environment of 2 gigabytes (WT2g) and the TREC-8 ad hoc topics were used, with normal ad hoc relevance assessment done for both the text and web collections. This allowed for "complete" judgment of the smaller web track against the ad hoc topics, but with more realistic web queries being used for the larger web collection [89].

Whereas this testing was initially only for efficiency (and various efficiency metrics were used in all three years), the use of web data as documents was also of interest. Like the speech data, web documents do not have a clear definition: in this case a document was defined as a single web document, including all of its parts but not including other documents linked to it. TREC-9 saw the introduction of the WT10g collection, a 10 gigabyte subset of the VLC2 corpus specifically constructed to mirror the web rather than simply being a large chunk of documents. There was a high degree of inter-server connectivity, along with other desirable corpus properties that were carefully preserved, creating a collection that was a proper testbed for web experiments [15]. Two years later a new collection (gov1) at 18 gigabytes was created from material in the *.gov domain [60].

Other than the vast scaling of the task, the web track up until 2000 (TREC-9) was still much in the Cranfield model. The initial topics were the ad hoc topics because a major goal of these experiments was to see how the scale and the structural information for the web documents affected "normal" ad hoc retrieval (it didn't much). However discussion with various web groups at this point made it very clear that the ad hoc topic style was only a small part of the web activity and if TREC wanted to reflect more realistic user models, the topics needed to change. So the TREC topics in 2000 looked for online services (such as ordering flowers), with short topics reverse-engineered from web query logs. The assessors selected topics from the search log and created a "full" TREC topic with description and narrative that matched *their* interpretation of that topic before examining the document set. The original log entry was included as the title of the new topic (with any original misspellings). This worked well in that the topic was well-enough defined to have consistent relevance judgments, but of a length that matched real web logs.

This reverse-engineering method continued to be used in the web track, but topics evolved into more specialized (and realistic) tasks in 2002, such as finding homepage locations and topic distillation (finding home-pages of relevant sites). The metrics also reflected this realistic model, with an emphasis on early success: success@1 (proportion of the queries with a good answer at rank 1), success@5 and success@10, and of course mean average precision just for comparison [61]. Starting in 2000 three-level judgments were used, again to reflect the web user model where web sites were likely to be highly relevant, relevant or non-relevant. The three-level judgment evaluation was effective, and in general the NIST assessors liked this mode of judgment because it made the decision process easier (personal communication from Ellen Voorhees). In 2004 there was a second web track called the Terabyte track, which used a much larger web collection, the 426 gigabyte"gov2" collection. This track is further discussed in Section 2.4.5.4.

In 2005 the original web track became the enterprise track, with the emphasis on looking at tasks more specific to intranet searching. Here the user model is someone within an organization searching in-house information. The data for 2005 and 2006 was a crawl of the W3C site, including email discussion lists, web pages and text in various formats. Topics were constructed for three search tasks: a known-item task (email message), an ad hoc search for email on a specific topic, and search for experts in a specific area [59]. Two of these tasks continued in 2006, but similar to earlier web track issues, there was concern that the topics/tasks being modeled were not realistic because they were being built by people outside of the organization. So in 2007 and 2008 the data *and* topics came from within one organization, CSIRO (Australian Commonwealth Scientific and Industrial Research Organization). The data was the CSIRO public web site, and the task that was modeled was that of creating a new "overview" page for a specific topic, which would include key links from the existing CSIRO web site along with key experts [17]. The CSIRO staff generated 50 such topics, with the track participants doing most of the relevance judging. For a discussion of how well this distributed judging worked, see [16].

## 2.4.4    DOMAIN-SPECIFIC RETRIEVAL TASKS

The tasks described in previous sections have all dealt with domain independent tasks: the data came from general news-type sources or from the web. With the possible exception of the enterprise track, where the user model required task-specific data, the domain of the documents did not influence the task. However some tracks in TREC have worked with domain-specific data, where the tasks and user models were driven by this data. One of the critical issues in dealing with domain-specific data is to determine the true information needs (and appropriate relevance criteria) for tasks within that domain. Note that in a minor way the Cranfield model was domain-specific in that the user model was defined as a scientist or engineer that might be searching in the domain of aerodynamics.

### 2.4.4.1   Genomics

Bill Hersh from Oregon Health Sciences Institute ran the genomics track for retrieval from medical information starting in TREC 2004. Part of the goal of this track was to see how well the ad hoc methods worked for the medical domain, but an additional part was to develop test collections and methodologies specifically suited to the retrieval needs of the genomics community. The document set for the first two years was 4 million MEDLINE records, about one-third the size of the full

MEDLINE database. Since these are basically abstracts but with many types of added metadata, the last two years of the track used 160,000 full-text papers from 49 genomics-related journals.

Whereas the data here was similar to the news-type sources, the selection of tasks and the building of the topic sets needed to closely mirror the requirements of the genomics community. In the first year, volunteers interviewed 43 genomic researchers, gathering 74 different information needs [93]. These were used to create 50 topics in a standard format similar to the ad hoc model. The task that year was a straight ad hoc task, using pooling and relevance judgments by people with medical backgrounds. The topics the second year were more focused, with six generic topic "templates" used to generate the 50 topics [92]. These templates allowed the topics to concentrate on known types of search problems, such as the role of a specific gene (where different genes could then be inserted in the template).

For the full-text documents for the next two years, the track moved to a passage retrieval task, e.g., find the relevant passages in the documents. Note that passages are difficult to define so this track had to create specific definitions, deal with the difficult relevance judgment issues that go with judging passage retrieval and finally use metrics that are appropriate for passage retrieval [131]. The passages were defined to have a maximum span of one paragraph, but could be much shorter, e.g., the minimum passage that would answer the topic/question. By the final year of the track (2007), a specific passage mean average precision (MAP) measure had been developed that compared character overlap between the submitted passages and those that had been selected as the "gold-standard" by the judges. A pooling mechanism was used with the passages, but then the submitted passages were judged not only for relevancy but their coverage of all the specific aspects of the answer. "To assess relevance, judges were instructed to break down the questions into the required elements (e.g., the biological entities and processes that make up the questions) and isolate the minimum contiguous substring that answered the question [96]." There was also an aspect-level MAP that looked at what percentage of the aspects were covered. The final evaluation used all three MAPs (document-level, passage-level and aspectual-level), making this one of the most complex evaluations at TREC.

### 2.4.4.2 Legal

The Legal track, started in 2006, resulted from a collaboration of information retrieval researchers with the legal community to "develop and apply objective criteria for comparing methods for searching large heterogeneous collections using topics that approximate how real lawyers would go about propounding discovery in civil litigation" [20]. This in turn was driven by new regulations governing how electronic data would be used in civil cases in federal courts. Doug Oard and David Lewis worked with Jason Baron of the U.S. National Archives and Records Administration to adapt traditional ad hoc testing methodology to this task.

The data collection was the IIT Complex Document Information Processing (CDIP) Test Collection [20] of about 7 million document records from the Legacy Tobacco Documents library. These documents, in the form of XML records, contain many kinds of electronic records such as email, OCR'd versions of tables and handwritten documents, etc., and therefore represent a challenge both in size and in "noise" levels.

The topics were uniquely created to mirror actual legal searches. The starting points were several (3 in 2008) hypothetical complaints, such as "a shareholder class action suit alleging securities fraud advertising in connection with a fictional tobacco company's campaign". These complaints were used to generate the traditional ad hoc topics (there were 45 in 2008). These complaints and the resulting topics were created by the Sedona Conference Working Group on Electronic Document Retention and Production, a nonprofit group of lawyers, who also then created the baseline Boolean queries for these topics. These Boolean queries would have been the "normal" way of requesting information in this type of legal situation. For more on this, including a deeper background of the legal process, see [20].

There were three tasks in 2008 and 2009 [91]: an ad hoc task, a relevance feedback task, and an interactive task. For the ad hoc task, systems returned both a ranked list and their optimal cutoff (K) on a per topic basis, with the main metric being the F measure at K. Although recall is critical to the legal profession, it is also important to return "good" sets as opposed to just ranked lists. The relevance judgments were made using enormous pools of documents, with various sampling methods tried in different years . The final set of documents (an average of over 500 per topic), were judged by volunteer second and third-year law students. (The interactive task was very user oriented and is discussed in Chapter 3 along with the other interactive tasks in TREC).

### 2.4.4.3  Blogs
Iadh Ounis and Craig Macdonald from the University of Glasgow worked with NIST to design and create a track dealing with the blogsphere in TREC2006. They created a large blog collection [126] containing 88.8GB of Permalinks, along with associated homepages, crawled from 100,649 blog feeds during an 11-week period. The crawl was specifically designed to include topics of interest to the NIST assessors and to include assumed spam blogs (splogs) to allow for realistic tasks. Note that whereas blogs are not a specific domain such as genomics and legal, they have a different nature (and often language) than newswire or web text, and attract different types of user tasks.

The blog track in TRECs 2006, 2007 and 2008 worked with opinion finding tasks, where the definition of a document was the blog post plus all the associated comments as identified by a Permalink. The task was to find all documents containing an opinion on a given topic, and then to identify if that opinion was positive, negative, or "mixed". The 50 topics were generated by the NIST assessors, using a query log from BlogPulse as seeds for reverse-engineering of the full topic. The documents were judged as: not relevant to the topic (0), relevant but not containing an opinion (1), relevant and containing a negative opinion (2), same as 2 but mixed opinion (3), and same as 2 but positive opinion (4). Traditional ad hoc metrics were used both on the relevancy (marked 1 or higher), and on the relevant including opinions (2 or higher) [127].

A second obvious task for blogs was the blog distillation task run in TRECs 2007 and 2008, where the user model is a person seeking to find an interesting blog to follow or read in their RSS reader. Here the documents were defined as the full blog, i.e., the aggregates of blog posts, and the topics were contributed and judged by the TREC participants. The guidelines for this were that the blog should be principally devoted to the given topic over the whole timespan of the collection.

The blog track in 2009 [120] had a much larger collection (Blogs08), with 28.5 million blog posts sampled from 1.3 million blog feeds from January 2008 to February 2009. A more complex distillation task required that systems use blog attributes (opinionated, personal, or in-depth) as well as the blog topic, with fifty topics developed and judged at NIST.

## 2.4.5    PUSHING THE LIMITS OF THE CRANFIELD MODEL

All of the test collections previously discussed were basically using the Cranfield model. Whereas the "documents" may be text, or speech, or websites, or blogs, and there were various user goals being modeled in the topics, the end result was usually a ranked list of unique items for judgment, and most of the collections could be considered re-usable. This final set of TREC tracks are grouped together because each of them required some major deviation from the Cranfield model, usually leading to either limitations on the resulting test collection or unsolved problems in the evaluation.

### 2.4.5.1   Question-Answering

The question-answering track, which ran for 9 years starting in 1999 (TREC-8), required systems to return *the answer* to a question instead of returning a ranked list of documents. This task both tested a new user model and created an opportunity to work with the natural language processing community. Whereas the document collections were the basic English ones used in the ad hoc task, the topics were questions, starting with simple fact-based, short answer questions (factoids) such as "How many calories in a Big Mac?", and progressing to "definition" questions such as "Who is Colin Powell?".

Note that the definition of a test collection had to be changed for this track. Whereas there are documents and topics/questions, the answer set is not the set of relevant documents, but rather "pieces" of one (or more) documents. In TRECs 8, 9 and 10, passages of lengths 250 and 50 words respectively were returned as the answers (along with the document id), and variable length strings were returned starting in 2002 [186].

The answer sets described above do not constitute a reusable test collection because the unit that is judged is only the answer string. Different runs seldom return exactly the same strings, and it is quite difficult to determine automatically if the difference between a new string and the judged string is significant with respect to the correctness of the answer. Any new system using this test collection is likely to return different answers which could be correct but would be "graded" wrong, making their experimental results not reliable. Whereas there is no known answer to this problem, NIST (and later Ken Litkowski) manually created answer patterns consisting of Perl string-matching algorithms from the answer strings [192] and researchers use these patterns along with the correct document ids to automatically score their new experiments (see software at `http://people.csail.mit.`

edu/gremio/code/Nuggeteer). Note that these are not truly correct scores (see [192] for more on this), but only approximations; clearly in violation of the Cranfield re-usable collection model!

Participants submitted questions the first year, however in the following years NIST created around 500 factoid questions using Excite logs as seeds, real questions from Encarta, and full questions coming from Microsoft and AskJeeves logs. The answer strings for the factoid questions were pooled and judged, with scoring based on mean reciprocal rank (MRR) similar to the known item searching for the OCR track. List questions were added, such as "Name 4 countries that can produce synthetic diamonds", which were not only graded for correctness but also for redundancy, with the score being accuracy (number of correct answers divided by the target number).

For TREC 2002 exact answers were required in order to "prove" that the systems knew the answer. Note that this would not be the actual user model, but could be considered as part of an interface where the exact answer would be highlighted in the text. Only one answer was allowed and the scoring was based on the number of correct answers using a new metric that also tested the confidence of the systems in their answers (see [186] for more details of this metric).

The last five years of the track had factoid, list and definition questions built in a series of questions such as a user might ask about a person, organization or a thing. For example, someone interested in the Hale Bopp comet might ask factoid questions such as "when was it discovered", list questions such as "what countries was it visible in on its last return", but also want to see "other" strings of interesting information. Whereas the factoid and list questions could be evaluated as before, the "other" strings required a new mechanism. The judging was done in two stages. In the first stage the assessors looked at a pool of all the system response strings and also added their own strings. These strings were then broken into "nuggets" for evaluation purposes, i.e., facts for which the assessor could make a binary decision as to whether a system response contained that nugget. Some of these nuggets were tagged as "vital", and systems were scored on recall (how many of the vital nuggets did they get), and precision, where precision was based on the length of the full set of strings (see [63, 182, 190] for more details).

### 2.4.5.2 Spam

The spam track was initiated in 2005 by Gordon Cormack of the University of Waterloo to encourage research in spam filtering. The major difficulty was the privacy issue since public distribution of personal email files is unethical and the few available public email files (such as the Enron data), or public forums do not accurately reflect real user experience. The track ran for 3 years, with a carefully constructed public corpus consisting of 75,419 messages (about two-thirds spam), and a private corpus from "MrX" consisting of 161,975 messages (95% spam). The public data from previous years could be used for training purposes, whereas the private corpus was accessed only via a toolkit that used 5 command-line operations (initialize, classify, train ham/spam, and finalize). The toolkit also was used in the evaluation to implement the various feedback tasks and to record and score results [58].

Four feedback tasks were designed to model different user behavior. The first gave immediate feedback, i.e., the correct answer was provided to the filter for quick "re-training". The second and third methods (delayed and partial) gave answers either at random times or for a subset of the messages. Finally, the active on-line learning task allowed participants to request answers for a small quota of the messages. The messages were presented for classification to the filters by the toolkit in a time-ordered fashion, with answers returned depending on the appropriate feedback task. After all messages had been classified, the scoring was based on ham misclassification and spam misclassification, with both ROC curves and a single metric (logistic average misclassification average provided (see [58] for definition of this metric).

### 2.4.5.3  Routing and Filtering Tasks

TREC also had a second type of task right from the beginning: the routing task. Here it was assumed that the user model is someone with an on-going information need, someone who has done some searching (and therefore has some relevant documents for their need), but wants to continue collecting more information. So the topic is fixed, but the document set keeps changing/growing. This user model certainly reflects an intelligence agent, but also news-clipping services, users following a particular news story, etc.

For the first 5 TRECs, the Cranfield model was essentially unchanged. The topics used were generally the ones from the previous TRECs, with the relevance judgments available, and the documents were some similar data that was specially gathered for the routing task. The results on the new data were submitted as a ranked list, then evaluated using the ad hoc pooling techniques and metrics. This scenario mostly worked, although at times it was difficult to find new data that matched the old topics, and participating systems tended to use this task as a way of improving their ad hoc results rather than thinking about a routing application.

It became clear by TREC-5 that this task did not reflect many user models; a more realistic task deals with filtering a time-ordered set of documents into a set of relevant ones for the user "inbox". This task could be modeled in several ways, such as in the batch filtering mode with "training" documents from one time-ordered set, and the test set from a later time-ordered set, or as an adaptive filtering task where training is incremental based on feedback from the user. However either case results in a set-based retrieval rather than a ranked list.

These tasks, started in TREC-6, and running for five years, along with the routing task, posed several big challenges in terms of evaluation [136]. The first was the continuing need to find reasonable data, and various options were tried, some more satisfactory than others. The final year TREC-11 (2002) [161] had a filtering collection specifically built for the Reuters collection using new TREC-style topics with a "complete" set of relevant documents formed by doing successive searching. It is *strongly* recommended that new filtering experiments use these 50 manually built topics from 2002, rather than the ones built for the earlier TREC filtering tracks. (Note however that there was also a set of 50 "experimental" topics built automatically in 2002 using the category tags from Reuters; these were not successful and should not be used.)

Another problem involved the pooling for relevance judging since the systems were not using ranked lists. Several methods were tried [118], such as sampling the results from each system and estimating the performance based on that sample, or sampling the pool of documents from all the systems. The fact that the routing task was continued in these years, allowing ranked list input to the pool somewhat helped the problem, but again, the 2002 filtering collection is strongly recommended because of its excellent set of judgments.

The final problem involved the metrics, which were generally utility measures. Note that because the systems are tuning on these metrics, one specific metric needs to be selected in advance, unlike the large range of metrics for the ad hoc task. Diverse utility measures were tried (again see [136]), including some F measures. The "correct" metric to use remains an unsolved problem as each metric reflects a different user model and the choice of the metric strongly effects both the results and the sampling methods that are used for pooling.

### 2.4.5.4 Terabyte, Million Query and the "new" Web Tracks

The Terabyte track started in TREC 2004, with the goal of working on a larger, very realistic web collection. The collection (GOV2) had 426 gigabytes crawled from U.S. government sites (the .gov sites), including extracted text from PDF, Word and postscript files. For the first year of the track, there were 50 ad hoc topics created in a similar manner to the original web track and the top 85 documents from each run were pooled for the relevance assessments. In 2005 and 2006 a named page finding task was also run, where the task was to find a particular page that a user might have found once and then tried to relocate (known item task with "near duplicates"). There was also an efficiency task.

Whereas the Terabyte track was a mainly scale-up of the old web track to a larger collection, it was suspected that the relevance judgments would not be "complete". A new measure *bpref* [35] specifically designed for incomplete collections was tried, and the pools were made larger (top 100 documents) in 2005. Additionally it was found [32, 47] that the pools were biased in that there was a very high occurrence of title words from the topics in the relevant documents. This means that runs using mostly title words could score higher than more "exotic" runs because documents without title words were simply not judged. This problem was likely caused by the huge scale of these collections, with many occurrences of relevant documents that never appear in the pools.

In 2006 the Terabyte track [37] made an effort to measure this effect by building three separate pools. The first pool (used for MAP evaluation) was the top 50 documents from each run. The second pool started at rank 400, selecting additional documents up to a total of 1000 documents per topic to gain some idea of how many additional relevant documents were not judged, with the metric being the *titlestat* measure [32]. Here it was found that there were indeed more relevant to be found at these deeper depths, with the titlestat measure still reading 0.6 at depths 400-500, down from 0.74 at depths 1-100. The third pool was a random sample using estimates of probability of relevance based on the relevance judgments from the first pool (top 50), and results of experiments done in 2006. This third pool was used for a new evaluation measure *inferred average precision, infAP* [202]. Three metrics for effectiveness were used in 2006: MAP, bpref and infAP.

Efforts to deal with the pooling problems led to the Million Query Track starting in 2007 [7]. The idea of this track was to investigate whether it was better to use many more queries/topics with shallow judgments rather than the more traditional pooling for 50 topics. There were 10,000 queries selected from a search engine log with the only requirement being that there was at least one click on the GOV2 corpus. In 2007 there were 1700 of these that were judged for 40 documents, where the judgments were done at NIST and by the participants. The queries to be judged were selected in a "quasi-random" manner, with the assessor picking a query from a set of 10 (or skipping to the next set), and then using that query as a seed to build a full TREC topic statement. The documents that were judged for each topic did not come from traditional pooling but were sampled using one of two different methods, Minimal Test Collections (MTC) [41] or statAP [12, 13], using the appropriate evaluation measures for the results.

The track in 2008 modified several parameters in order to more deeply investigate these two methods. The 10,000 queries were equally divided into four sets: those with 6 or fewer words that had fewer than 3 clicks in GOV2, those with more words and more clicks, and the other two possibilities (few clicks/long query, more clicks/short query). The judgments were done only at NIST, with 792 queries judged for up to five different stopping points (8, 16, 32, 64, and 128 judgments). This allowed a finer-grained investigation of the strengths and weaknesses of the two different methods. It was found [6] that the MAPs were more stable using MTC for the smaller number of judgments (16/32), whereas statAP was more stable for 64/128 judgments. However MTC seemed more affected by the different query categories.

Both the Million Query and Terabyte (renamed Web) tracks continued in 2009 using a new collection ClueWeb09 (http://boston.lti.cs.cmu.edu/Data/clueweb09). This collection consists of roughly 1 billion web pages (25TB of uncompressed data) in multiple languages resulting from a crawl during January and February 2009. A smaller subset (Category B) of the collection consists of 50 million documents which are approximately the first 50 million English documents hit by the crawl plus the English version of Wikipedia. It should be noted that the Category B subcollection has many unique characteristics, including high-quality "seed" documents that were used to generate the rest of the crawl and results from this subcollection (or any subset of a large web collection) need to be carefully considered with respect to any conclusions or generalizations not tested on the full set. The web track in 2009 had an ad hoc task (50 topics using MTC pooling and evaluation), and a pilot diversity task where documents were also judged with respect to special subtopic fields.

## 2.5    OTHER EVALUATION CAMPAIGNS

Since 1992 there have been other evaluation campaigns, often starting in a similar vein as TREC and then branching out into new areas especially appropriate for their participants. In addition to the three discussed here, there is the FIRE evaluation (http://www.isical.ac.in/) with a concentration of work with various Indian languages and the Russian evaluation (http://romip.ru/en/).

## 2.5.1   NTCIR

An Asian version of TREC (NTCIR) started in 1999, with the conferences occurring every 18 months since then. Whereas NTCIR has run evaluations in a similar mode to TREC, there has always been a tighter connection to the NLP community, allowing for some unique tracks. Additionally NTCIR pioneered retrieval evaluations with patents, developing appropriate evaluation techniques for searching, classification, and translation efforts in this field. Online proceedings and more information about NTCIR can be found at `http://research.nii.ac.jp/ntcir`.

This first NTCIR (August 1999) worked with 339,483 Japanese abstracts from 65 Japanese academic societies; about half of these abstracts were also in English, and all were written by the authors. The 83 Japanese topics were gathered from researchers, with assessments done via pooling and at three levels (relevant, partially relevant and non-relevant). NTCIR-2 (March 2001) had a similar task, with the same collection but with the 49 new topics also translated to English (allowing CLIR from English to Japanese) and a fourth grade for relevance judgments (highly relevant).

By NTCIR-3 (October 2002) there were three languages for CLIR, with over two hundred thousand newspaper articles in Japanese and Chinese from 1998-1999, plus a smaller collection in Korean. Topics were built in four languages (including English), and were translated for the other languages, with tags in the topics to indicate both the source language and the target (translated) language. Note that because trec_eval was not set up for graded relevance judgments, there was a "rigid relevant" (highly relevant and relevant) score and a "relaxed relevant" (also including partial relevant) score. More newspapers were added in NTCIR-4 (June 2004), making almost equally sized collections for Japanese, Chinese, Korean and English (from English versions of Asian newspapers). The compatibility of the document sets across all four languages allowed complete multilingual testing to be done, and this continued in NTCIR-5 (December 2005) with new document sets from the 2000-2001 timeframe.

The NTCIR-6 (May 2007) CLIR task was run in two stages and without the English documents. In stage one there were 140 topics reused from NTCIR-3 and 4, but this time against the newer document sets from 2000-2001. Only shallow pools of the top 10 documents per run were judged, and 50 of the topics having enough relevant documents were used in the scoring. In addition to the rigid and relaxed scores, the multi-grade relevance scoring (nDCG and Q) was used. Stage 2 was a rerun of the NTCIR-6 systems, without parameter adjustment, on the NTCIR-3 thru 5 test collections. The goal of stage 2 was to provide information for cross-collection analysis.

The NLP connection in NTCIR encouraged both a summarization task (NTCIR-2-NTCIR-4) and a question answering task. The summarization task was done in Japanese only; looking at single and multiple document summaries of newspapers. Different evaluation methods were tried, including comparing the submitted summaries on a scale from 1-4 (best to worst) for completeness and readability and counting the number of character edits (insertion, deletions, substitutions) that were needed to turn the automatic summary into the human summary. The question answering task was also done in Japanese only and was similar to the TREC 2002 QA task in that exact answers were required for the 200 questions. However a subtask consisted of 40 "followup" questions, where a question related to one of the 200 initial questions asked for more information using pronouns or ellipsis. This task continued in NTCIR 4 and 5 with series questions, but became a cross-language QA task starting in NTCIR-6.

The cross-language effort and the question-answering effort merged into one task in NTCIR-7 and 8, allowing for component-based evaluation in both the retrieval and the question components, plus providing a platform for exchanging interim results and combining modules for different systems.

NTCIR has had a major patent retrieval task since NTCIR-3 [71]. The first year the task was a technology survey using search topics inspired by newspaper articles in four languages against two years of Japanese patents with the goal of finding relevant patents. This task became a true patent invalidity task in NTCIR-4, against ten years of Japanese patents, including major experimentation into how to get large number of topics (invalid patents) more easily by using the rejection citations as the relevant documents. This method was enhanced in NTCIR-5, along with including a subtask using passages as opposed to full documents. NTCIR-6 (2007) saw more emphasis on CLIR in patents, with both a Japanese patent invalidity task and an English one using 10 years of U.S. Patent data. A translation task was added in NTCIR-7 and 8, including an aligned corpus of these patents. Patent classification has also been evaluated, along with assignment of patent classification codes to research papers, both monolingually in Japanese and English, and in a cross-language mode.

## 2.5.2    CLEF

The European CLIR task moved from TREC to a new conference, CLEF (Cross-Language Evaluation Forum) in 2000. Whereas one of the reasons for the move was that TREC needed to work on non-European languages, the major reason was that it become obvious that U.S. participants did not have the background (nor maybe the interest) to progress much further in the research. The European partners who had worked with TREC were interested in starting a new conference, led by Carol Peters of CNR Pisa, not only to continue the European CLIR effort but to expand it to more languages and more participants from Europe. Working notes from all of the CLEF workshops can be found at `http://www.clef-campaign.org/`, with formal proceedings produced in the Springer Lecture Notes in Computer Science each year.

In 2000 there were the initial four TREC languages (English, French, German and Italian), however, each year thereafter saw the addition of one or two new languages, starting with Spanish and Dutch in 2001, and eventually ending with 13 different languages for the documents, and even more languages for the topics. In order for a new language to be added, a native-speaking support group from that country needed to obtain adequate newspaper data from the 1994/1995 period, arrange for the data to be put in TREC-like formatting, and then provide personnel to create topics, perform relevance judgments, etc. This was a major effort and it is a credit to the CLIR community that so many groups were able to do this. As languages were added, research groups in the new language area were able to perform their research using their own language for the first time as monolingual ad hoc retrieval tasks were offered in these new languages. Additionally the cross-language effort (bilingual and multilingual) was continued, with a main task of retrieving documents across 8 different languages, a smaller task of using only 4 languages (English, French, German and Spanish), and then different specific bi-lingual pairs, such as Finnish to German, Italian to Spanish, French to Dutch, etc. Not all language pairs were offered in a given year in order to concentrate the effort of the participants. The expansion of the CLEF CLIR ad hoc tasks into so many languages not only enabled many new research groups to join in, but for the first time allowed major investigations into the differences between languages with respect to retrieval [155].

There were several specific evaluation issues given the widespread distributed nature of the CLEF evaluation effort. First, topic creation needed to be managed very carefully to truly reflect the user model. The initial topics needed to mirror the types of questions asked within the various countries, and this was done (for example) in CLEF 2001 by asking each of the 5 language groups that year to generate a set of 15 topics, along with doing a pre-search to make sure the topics were covered in each of the 5 languages [201]. These 75 initial topics were then jointly pruned to 50 topics based on potential problems in one or more of the languages. The final set of topics was then translated directly to the other languages, with indirect use of the English master set only when necessary. Note that it is critical that the translation not be word-for-word, but take into account both the linguistic and the cultural background of the target languages, i.e., the final topics must represent how a user in a given country would actually ask that question.

Another issue for CLEF was pooling given the sparse nature of the submissions. For example, in 2003, the first year for Finnish and Swedish, there were only 7 groups for Finnish and 8 for Swedish. A "uniques" test was performed [30] to check for the completeness of the resulting test collection. This test involves creating multiple sets of relevance judgments, actually *n+1* sets containing the original (full) set plus *n* sets built by removing those relevant documents uniquely found by one participating group. These *n+1* sets are then each used to create the test results, with the goal of showing how a given group would have performed if their unique relevant documents had not been in the pool, i.e., not considered relevant. The results for Finnish and Swedish showed a maximum drop in performance of 0.31% for Finnish and 2.02% for Swedish, which can be considered not significant.

CLEF also attracted many new tracks over the years, such as cross-language question answering (24 groups doing working in 10 languages against target text of 9 languages in 2005), a geospatial track specifically looking at topics with geospatial information, and a structured data track (GIRT) using structured documents in 3 languages. One of the more unusual (and popular) tracks was ImageCLEF, which started work with captioned photographs in 2003, where the goal was to search topics built in 5 languages against the English captions. This track expanded to include over 20,000 "touristic" photographs with captions in English, German and Spanish, along with 50,000 medical images with annotations in several languages. Whereas the initial and continued main task was work with the captions, eventually the images themselves were also used in the retrieval task, either alone or in combination with the captions.

### 2.5.3   INEX

The INitiative for the Evaluation of XML retrieval (INEX) started in 2002 to provide evaluation of structured documents, in particular to investigate retrieval of document components that are XML elements of varying granularity. The initiative used 12,107 full-text scientific articles from 18 IEEE Computer Society publications, with each article containing 1,532 XML nodes on average. The collection grew to 16,819 articles in 2005 and moved on to using Wikipedia articles starting in 2006. Like its sister evaluations, INEX has also had auxiliary "tracks" over the years (see `http://inex.is.informatik.uni-duisburg.de/` for INEX through 2007; the current site is `http://www.inex.otag.nz/`).

The main task of ad hoc retrieval has run since the beginning but with major differences from TREC, NTCIR, and CLEF. Because the goal is retrieval of a particular element of the document that is demarcated by XML tags, the "relevant" documents can range from a paragraph to the whole document. The general idea has been to present the user with the "best" element in the article with respect to their information request, that is an element that exhaustively discusses the topic without including too many irrelevant topics. The notions of exhaustivity and specificity, although well known to the information retrieval community, are very difficult to measure, and this has caused extensive investigations of new metrics within INEX over the years [114]. This difficulty also extends to the relevance assessments and is part of the reason that all of the relevance assessments in INEX are done by the participants.

The ad hoc topics in INEX (also built by the participants) have reflected the structural nature of the task. The content-only (CO) topics resemble TREC topics, however the content-and-structure (CAS) topics include NEXI query language in the title section, which provides specific structural criteria. Results from both kinds of topics have been evaluated similarly, although the structural constraints in the CAS topics were interpreted variously.

The 2007 ad hoc track illustrates the complexity of the evaluation. There were four subtasks with different sets of results: thorough (ranked list of elements), focused (ranked list of focused non-overlapping elements), relevant in context (ranked list of the full articles, but including a set of non-overlapping elements), and best in context (ranked list of the articles, but including the best entry point). Each task models a different user approach, with the focused assuming a top-down look across the ranked elements, and the relevant in context and best in context assuming the user wants to see the full document, but with more complex displays for the elements within that document.

There were 4 additional tracks in 2005, building up to 8 tracks plus ad hoc by 2009, with the common thread being the use of XML. The longer running tracks have been interactive (user studies for XML documents), multimedia (retrieving images using the XML structures), and document mining (clustering and classification of XML structured documents). A book search track for digitized books, entity ranking and question answering within the XML environment started in 2007. Because the data is Wikipedia, there is a Link-the-Wiki track, and also an efficiency track.

## 2.6 FURTHER WORK IN METRICS

There has been considerable interest and work on new metrics since 1992, coming from perceived needs of TREC and other evaluations, but also from the explosion of information access available today. Since the emphasis in this chapter has been more on the design of test collections, this section is only a brief summary of the new metrics; for a much more detailed discussion, see [147].

By TREC-2 the new trec_eval was in place using non-interpolated average precision and the new R-precision (see section 2.3.2). But the known-item searching in the TRECs 5 and 6 OCR and speech tracks required another new metric, *mean-reciprocal-rank, MRR*, to allow proper averaging. MRR is the mean of the reciprocal of the rank where the known item was found, averaged across all the topics, and is mathematically equivalent to the mean average precision when there is only one target document [183].

The various web tracks have required new metrics, both because of the different tasks and because of the scaling issues for pooling. See the Terabyte track, Section 2.4.5.4, for discussion of the various metrics.

Another of the issues in TREC has been the averaging of results across the topics, even though there are wide variations in system performance when results are examined on a per topic basis. The statistical testing such as the t-test used earlier (see Chapter 5 in [147] for a excellent discussion of the use of statistics in information retrieval evaluation) is one possible way of examining these effects. However a new metric *GMAP* using the geometric mean of the average precision scores (as opposed to the arithmetic mean) was used in a variation of the ad hoc track in 2004 to emphasize success on the "harder" topics [187].

The final metric briefly covered in this section was not driven by TREC issues but by a general awareness that binary relevance judgments were not sufficient and that some type of grading of judgments was needed (similar to what is done for commercial search engines). The group at Tampere University [99] devised a framework for dealing with graded relevance judgments *Discounted Cumulative Gain, DCG* which uses both the relevance grades and the position on the document ranking to give a single score. This can be parameterized to give more or less discounting. A normalized version of this (nDCG) [100] is heavily used both in commercial search engine evaluations and in other evaluations having graded relevance assessing. The measure has also been recently adapted to handle multi-query sessions [101] and diverse query evaluation [46].

## 2.7 SOME ADVICE ON USING, BUILDING AND EVALUATING TEST COLLECTIONS

This final section departs from the more formal coverage of the batch evaluations by offering some advice on selecting appropriate test collections, building new test collections, and evaluating those collections. This advice is not meant to be a complete manual on this topic but rather comes from personal observations during many years of working with test collections.

## 2.7.1    USING EXISTING COLLECTIONS

The easiest evaluation method for batch experiments is to use an existing collection. This method not only cuts the major costs of building a collection, but also provides training material. An equally important issue is the universal acceptance of these test collections, including the ability to compare results to other work. However this decision should not be taken automatically; the user task and the assumptions about the users should be appropriately matched to the selected test collection and test collection characteristics need to be considered in any analysis of the results.

The most heavily used test collections for monolingual English retrieval are the TREC ad hoc ones. These collections are based on mainly on newspapers and newswires, along with government documents. The topics are general-purpose and domain-independent, and there is a reasonable assumption that the relevance judgments are complete. But there are 9 sets of topics (1-450), searched against different document sets, so which to pick? The best choice for most experiments are the 3 sets used in TRECs 6-8, consisting of 150 topics (numbers 301-450) searched against (mostly) the same data (disks 4 and 5). This set provides 150 topics, enough for good statistical analysis, plus this group is the most consistent in terms of topic format and relevance judgments.

Some of the earlier TREC ad hoc collections need to be used with caution. Topics 1-50, used for minimal training in TREC-1, are poor topics with only minimal relevance judgments. Topics 51-150, used in TRECs 1 and 2 have an expanded format; this may be useful for particular kinds of experiments, such as structured query experiments, however the topics themselves were created in a possibly unnatural manner, with the relevance judgments being done by another person. Topics 150-200 (TREC-3), were constructed with reference to the documents, and because they often use terms from the documents, are the "easiest" of the TREC topic sets. Topics 201-250 for TREC-4 have no narrative field, which may or may not be necessary depending on the experiment.

Other TREC track test collections are also available (http://trec.nist.gov/data.html), including test collections for OCR and speech, non-English ad hoc collections, and collections for web, blog, genomics, legal, etc. Whereas the Chinese and European language collections are available (the Chinese one for TREC-6 is not recommended because of issues with the topic building process), it is better to get the NTCIR and CLEF collections for these languages. The Arabic collections (TRECs 2001 and 2002) are available at NIST, although the second one (2002) is the recommended one since the improved systems meant better pooling. Other collections are also available, usually with the topics and other auxiliary data on the TREC web site and a pointer to the documents which are available elsewhere. Note however that these collections are all specialized, based on possibly narrower tasks and/or user models and these issues should be thoroughly understood (by reading track overviews about the collection characteristics) before using these collections.

What about using the much older small collections? These collections are much too small for testing and validating new technology; furthermore most of them use abstracts rather than full documents and results may well be misleading because of this. However one exception to this would be to use them (particularly the TIME collection) as teaching tools; but here again the benefits of a much smaller collection for failure analysis need to be weighed against the different insights one gains when working on the larger collections.

## 2.7.2   SUBSETTING OR MODIFYING EXISTING COLLECTIONS

Another option is to subset an existing collection or modify it to better fit an experiment. Many of the collections are small and therefore cannot be subset in terms of topics, however one could concentrate on subsets of the documents. For example groups have studied the effects of hyphenation and effective retrieval of long structured Federal Register (FR) documents [199]. Other characteristics of the data such as spelling errors (especially in newswires), duplication of information (again mostly in newswires), British vs. American English (FT vs. WSJ), evolution over time of news stories, and other areas invite further study. Additionally some sources of documents provide fielded information ranging from titles and headlines to manual indexing terms to the heavily structured data in the patent collection. Any of these ideas could be used to generate subcollections of documents, however care needs to be taken that there are enough documents in the subset to generate valid results and any possible biases introduced in this subsetting need to be considered in result analysis.

Modifying a collection is more difficult and (possibly) loses some of the advantages of using an existing collection. One obvious modification would be to change the relevance judgments, either by changing the unit of judgment (doing passage retrieval for example) or by changing the definition of relevance. The TREC relevance judgments for the ad hoc task are the broadest type of judgments, i.e., the fact that a document contained ANY information about a topic/question was enough to make it relevant. This was important because the perceived definition of the TREC task/user was that of a high-recall task. But it also was important in terms of creating the most complete set of relevance judgments possible. The current judgments could be used as the starting point for other types of relevance judgments, such as removal of "duplicate" documents [24], or the use of graded relevance judgments [99, 162] or even the measurement of some type of learning effect (the TREC novelty track). This type of modification is very tricky; in essence a second relevance judgment is being made, with all of the consistency difficulties discussed earlier, which may affect the experiment. For some discussion of the problems, see [81, 203].

## 2.7.3   BUILDING AND EVALUATING NEW AD HOC COLLECTIONS

Building a new collection is a major step to take; it is costly in terms of time and money and full of pitfalls for those new to this task. However if it is to be done, then the critical thing is that the experiments and the new collection they use be modeled on some real user task and that the characteristics of likely users be considered as part of this task. Are the users searching the web for a nearby restaurant with good reviews, are they searching their company's intranet for patents, or are they browsing the web for information about some specific type of tree they want to plant? Each of these applications requires a different set of documents, different types of "topics", different definitions of relevance, and different types of metrics to use in evaluation. These decisions need to be made long before the collection is built.

Once this piece of the design is done, then the next step is to find some documents. Again the easiest place to start would be some existing set of documents that can either be used as is or be subsetted in some manner. Possibly the news collections from TREC/NTCIR/CLEF are useful, but more likely the new web collection (`http://boston.lti.cs.cmu.edu/Data/clueweb09`), or the blog collection [120] are candidates. Note that any sub-setting of these collections needs to be done carefully; both the blog and web collections were carefully sampled during their construction process and any subsets need to reflect the new user task design being envisioned. The small web collection [89] design gives some clues on how to do this, the construction of the WT10g [15] also discusses web collection design or see the discussion of the recent "Category B" of the ClueWeb09 collection. Note that subsets of these collections cannot be re-distributed, however one could make subsets using the "docids" for reuse by others. If completely new document sets need to be collected (a major job), then hopefully this can be done in some manner so that the work can be used by others. This means that any intellectual property rights need to be resolved and that the data has to be formatted for ease of use.

Given that the documents are collected, the next step is the topics. Again the user task/characteristics need to be modeled; ideally some real topics from a log can be gathered, or some topics can be built by "surrogate" users such as those used in the TREC/NTCIR/CLEF ad hoc tasks. Enough topics need to be built to overcome topic variation in performance [188, 189]; 25 can be taken to be the absolute minimum, with 50 a more reasonable number. The format of the topics needs to mirror the task; for example browsing the web looking for a specific item may need a series of related topics to mimic the interactive search process. Topics for a specific domain need to be appropriate for that domain, either by getting domain experts to build the topics (such as the legal track), or by using a survey such as that done before topic construction by the genomics track to gather representative needs of the genomics community. It is equally critical to closely examine the issues with searching a given genre, such as the patent tracks in NTCIR, TREC and CLEF. The NTCIR efforts in multiple years have tackled different pieces of the patent retrieval problem, but all based on realistic analysis of the needs of that community [71]. If multiple languages are involved, then the topics need to be constructed so that there is no bias towards one language [201].

The methodology for making the relevance judgments for the topics is again reliant on the user task and characteristics. Does the user want only document level judgments or are passage (or even sentence) level judgments needed (such as for genomics and question-answering)? What types of judgments are required (binary, graded or other), how many judgments per topic (a major cost factor), and of course setting up the mechanics of getting the documents to judge (pooling, manual search, or some other method such as the sampling done in the TREC Million Query Track). Many different approaches to pooling have been tried over the years (see section 6.3 in [147]), each with some advantages and weaknesses that need to be considered in light of the goals of the test collection. Finally, of course, the judging needs to be done.

Once the collection is built, some types of validation need to be made. If this collection is used only for a single experiment, the validation is needed only to understand any likely biases that affect the analysis of the results. However if the test collection can be used by others, then some measures must be made of the consistency and completeness of the relevance judgments (see section 2.3.2 in this lecture or Chapter 6 in [147]).

### 2.7.4    DEALING WITH UNUSUAL DATA

The previous section built on the assumption that the test collection is a "standard" collection working with textual documents, but many interesting applications have more diverse data. For example, the TREC speech retrieval task (and the video retrieval task) not only worked with multi-media data but had to define the "boundaries" of the documents. Here, and also in the blog track, these definitions were coordinated with the specific task being modeled, with a document defined as the blog post plus all the associated comments as identified by a Permalink for opinion finding, but defined as the full blog (the aggregates of blog posts) for the blog distillation task. In both cases the definition of a document was based on the output a user might expect to see for these tasks. This was also the basis for the various versions of the question-answering track, and for the passage retrieval part of the genomics track.

It can be the situation that the data to be searched has a major impact on the tasks; this is clearly true of the various TREC web/enterprise tracks, but also true of the NTCIR patent tasks. There the patent data had multiple fields and was multi-lingual, leading to a series of different tasks including cross-language retrieval to related newspaper articles in four languages, patent invalidity tasks, patent classification tasks, and patent translation tasks. The ImageCLEF track in CLEF started with captioned black&white images, where the major emphasis was on using the captions, moved to color photographs with multilingual captions where the images became equally important, and tackled a series of medical retrieval tasks with x-rays. In each of these cases the data determined the task; a similar situation occurs in the TRECvid evaluations. INEX has worked with semi-structured data, including books, Wikipedia, etc., with the tasks, topics, and metrics highly influenced by the data to be searched.

### 2.7.5    BUILDING WEB DATA COLLECTIONS

The TREC terabyte and web track built test collections based on the assumed needs of the TREC research community. The documents (web) were basically what could be obtained, and the topics and relevance assessments changed over the years to allow different research "themes" to be investigated. However the commercial search engines also build test collections, where they have the luxury of the full web, a real set of questions, plus other interesting metadata about searching. There is little information about how this is done, although Chapter 3 of this lecture has a discussion of the work done in the mining of search logs.

A paper presented at SIGIR in 2009 [122] provides one example of how this was done at Yahoo. The document collection is the entire web (at some given time). The query collection has 22,822 queries, randomly sampled from some population. A similar collection built by Microsoft [198] had 10,680 unique query statements taken from interaction logs where the users had provided consent to participate in this study (likely a similar case from the Yahoo test collection). In both these cases, the URLs of the retrieved documents were available. The Yahoo test collection had judgments for an average of 23 URLs for each query, done by human editors (not the users), on a rating of Perfect, Excellent, Good, Fair and Bad. The Microsoft collection also had relevance judgments (assigned on a 6-pt scale) by trained judges for those documents the users had examined during the study (note that this is going to be a special subset of the retrieved).

Both of these test collections emphasized large numbers of topics with shallow relevance judging, and likely the collections were built specifically for the given experiments. The metrics used depended on the goal of the experiments but they were all either high precision metrics or some form of graded relevance metrics. The huge amount of other metadata collected for the searches (see examples in Chapter 3 and in [175]) allows combining the relevance judgments with other information such as assigning grades based on what percentage of the user population clicked on this answer.

# CHAPTER 3

# Interactive Evaluation

## 3.1 INTRODUCTION

Information retrieval systems are built for users and it is critical to examine how the various information retrieval techniques (such as those evaluated by the batch retrieval methods) perform in operational settings. Conversely it is important to observe users in an information seeking task and then attempt to model how users behave in order to devise new retrieval techniques. This chapter looks at evaluation issues in user studies, with an emphasis on those studies aimed at understanding user behavior rather than testing the usability of systems. The chapter starts with a short review of evaluation in early user studies, followed by a discussion of the evaluation experiences in the interactive track in TREC. The third section is a look at some recent user studies, with the goal of examining how the high-level issues of experimental design affect the outcome of the final evaluations. The final section presents work using the massive log files from search engines, again with an emphasis on how the design of the experiment, including the selection of which log files to study, how to filter the files, etc. enable user behaviors to be teased out of that data.

It should be noted that the scope of this chapter is narrow; the recent tutorial (Methods for Evaluating Interactive Information Systems with Users) by Diane Kelly [111] provides detailed methodologies for organizing user studies, data collection and analysis techniques, etc. This lecture is meant to be a complement to that tutorial, examining the bridge between evaluation in user studies and in the batch laboratory mode. Other references for user studies are the recent book by Ingwersen and Järvelin [98] which presents frameworks for evaluation of various information seeking tasks, and the special issue of Information Processing and Management [28] on evaluation of interactive information retrieval systems.

## 3.2 EARLY WORK

Most of the early user studies involved either indexers or search intermediaries, the only users of retrieval systems at that time. Indeed the Cranfield I experiment discussed in Chapter 1 looked into different characteristics of indexers, including the knowledge of the subject matter being indexed and the level of general indexing experience. Both the Medlars study and the Case Western study also discussed in that chapter draw the clear conclusion that "human error" is the cause of various search failures, either at the indexing stage, or at the search construction stage. However this might be better called "human variation" since the issue is not one of error but rather a mismatch of search terms and document terms (index terms in this case), a scenario very familiar to today's searchers.

Michael Keen (earlier associated with both the Cranfield work and the SMART work) continued investigations into indexing. His first experiment looked at five different types of indexing languages in eight test comparisons to study specificity and language, specificity and exhaustivity, methods of co-ordination, and precision devices [105]. There were 800 documents, 72 requests from real users, and full relevance judgments using library staff. But in this experiment the searching was done in a less constrained manner by library science students, who were allowed a maximum of 40 minutes to search and were given a specific recall/precision target. A Latin Square design (see [111] for more information on Latin Square designs) was used so that each of the searchers processed each request once, but eventually used all of the different indexes, manually recording their searches for later analysis.

His followup experiment [109] emphasized the searchers' role, this time using different types of printed indexes and allowing complete freedom of search. The aim "was to test the effects of index entry variations on performance from the user's viewpoint", and 9 entry types were selected based on an extensive survey of printed indexes. These entry types involved features such as index term context, entry term order, and number of access points, and looked at constructions like lead term, KWOCs or KWACs. A subset of 50 requests, and 392 documents from the earlier testing was used, along with the earlier relevance judgments. The searchers were asked to "imagine that they were in a real-world search situation, to simulate delegated searches by subject experts, where a few relevant entries were required rapidly, and the search subsequently broadened, within a time limit of ten minutes for each search". The searchers kept extensive records of their search, including timing and relevance ratings, and annotated the index entry forms to track what they were using for the search. This was supplemented by audio recordings (think-alouds), with all this material then analyzed to provide not only some answers to what types of index entry forms were most useful, but also some insights into the mental processes of the search operations.

Note however that this set of experiments, and other similar experiments looking at the search intermediaries, were not addressing the "real" user of the system. It was assumed that the end users brought their information needs to a human search intermediary, who constructed a search (usually a series of searches) against some online data base such as MEDLINE or DIALOG. Taylor's prescient paper [174] explored how to better help end users by examining the user/search intermediary interaction, in particular noting that a user's initial question was "ambiguous, imprecise, and requires feedback from the system or from a colleague in order to provide an acceptable answer". Nick Belkin, working on a PhD in the late 1970s also wondered how end users might better communicate their information needs either to the intermediary or to a system directly. His ASK (Anomalous State of Knowledge) hypothesis was "that an information need arises from a recognized anomaly in the user's state of knowledge concerning some topic or situation and that, in general, the user is unable to specify precisely what is needed to resolve that anomaly" [23]. He further hypothesized [22] that these ASKs would fall into various classes requiring different types of retrieval strategies, and that a major goal of any information retrieval system would be to decide which types of strategies would be effective.

He and Bob Oddy did a design study [23] to test this model by tape recording interviews with 35 users of the Central Information Services of the University of London and then turning their stated information needs into structural representations of that ASK. Whereas the majority of this research involved creating these ASK structures, creating document structures and doing some type of matching, the research was the one of first to look in detail at these end user information needs. A summary of Table 6 of [23] gives five different ASK types based on these interviews, and the results are very similar to what is seen today.

A. Well-defined topic and problem

B. Specific topics. Problem well defined. Information wanted to back up research and/or hypotheses

C. Topics quite specific. Problem not so well defined. Research still at an early stage.

D. Topics fairly specific. Problems not well defined. No hypotheses underlying research

E. Topics and problems not well defined. Topics often unfamiliar.

By the early 1980s the end users were finally getting a chance to search on their own, with some of the larger libraries creating online versions (called OPACs) of their card catalogs. For example the MELVYL system at the University of California, Berkeley had a prototype online catalog of MARC records from all University of California campuses available to their library staff in 1980 and opened it to library patrons in 1981. In 1982 the National Library of Medicine (NLM) actually user tested [157] two different prototype access systems to their CATLINE online catalog, which contained over 500,000 records at the time of the study. One of the systems, CITE [64, 65] incorporated natural language input and ranking similar to the SMART system, with the other being a more conventional Boolean system (the ILS system). The user testing was done in three stages, with the CITE system available from late April through May, and the ILS system available from June through August. Over 600 surveys asked users about the amount of information retrieved, the system response time and user satisfaction with both the results and the system . Additionally 60 randomly selected library patrons used both systems (controlled as to order) before taking the survey. Siegel [157] noted that "the three studies of user acceptance yield strong and consistent patterns of user preferences, which were separately corroborated by the results of technical testing." CITE was the system was overwhelmingly preferred and was used as NLM's online catalog system for 2 or 3 years until replaced by Grateful Med (personal communication from Tamas Doszkocs).

As more OPACs came into being, more user studies were done, with user surveys being supplemented by transaction log analysis. Tolle [176] reported on work done with logs obtained from six libraries, including the NLM CATLINE (8 weeks of 441,282 transactions from over 11 thousand users), with the specific types of data collected including the terminal identification, the system used, the file searched, user commands, times of starting and finishing, and the system response. The data from these logs was mapped into 11 primary user action states, such as start of session, set creation/searching, display of records, access to help functions, and errors that occurred. These states were then used to construct a state transition matrix, which could be analyzed to answer specific questions. For example it was found that errors tend to occur in clusters (high probability of transition to a second error), and that subject searches could result in zero hits in over 50% of the sessions. Borgman [27] contrasted user behavior in both bibliographic databases (such as DIALOG), mainly used by professional searchers, and the public OPACs, noting for example that OPAC users are mostly infrequent users who quit searching almost 20% of the time after the first error (9% of their input). Even once past the error barrier, these users had trouble using the Boolean logic, particularly in subject searching, which constituted over 50% of the searches.

The access problems of OPAC users attracted researchers in the 1980s, in particular a group at the Polytechnic of Central London library. A series of retrieval experiments [132], evaluated within an OPAC operational setting (the Okapi system), took place starting in 1984 [123], examining the effects of system changes on user search performance. Note that most subject searching based on keywords then had an implicit "AND" operator between input terms, causing massive failures (34% of 1000 subject searches with no records found [196]). Therefore the first Okapi experiment tried a best match system, with ranking based on relative term frequency in the index (a variation of IDF). The evaluation on a single terminal in the library included 70 structured interviews (user background, what they were searching for, and comments on Okapi), plus transaction logging from which 96 user sessions could be clearly isolated. In general users liked the new system, but it was found that only 38% of the searches were subject searches rather than for specific items (title/author) and that the average number of terms per subject search was just over two.

The Okapi 1987 experiments [196] investigated stemming and spelling correction since transaction logs from the 1984 Okapi system revealed that more than 25% of the subject searches would have been helped by simple stemming, and about 10% of the searches containing unnoticed spelling errors. Two versions of the system were installed on alternative days on two terminals at the library, with about 120 users interviewed over a one month period. The two versions were a control (CTL) system with weak stemming (including an "s" stemmer and "ed" / "ing" verb stems), and an experimental system (EXP) with a strong stemmer (Porter), spelling correction and a lookup table for phrases and equivalence classes of related terms. The evaluation involved both observation/interviews and transaction log analysis. The observations were mostly to note problems and to collect beginning and end session times, with the interviews asking about frequency of catalog use, what was the target of the search, the success of the search and any problems encountered. The transaction logs allowed the experimenters to repeat the exact (initial) search, on either of the two test systems or on a system with no stemming (the original system). It is worth noting that this two-stage approach was deemed necessary because earlier pilot studies had shown that most searches would return the same documents regardless of the system and therefore a direct comparison of the two systems (such as that done for the CITE system at NLM) would not have been sensitive enough to find differences. Indeed the results bore this out; even though the weak stemming retrieved more records in almost half of the initial searches repeated from the transaction logs, it "rarely turned a search from a complete failure into a success", and the strong stemming hurt performance as much as it helped.

A third set of experiments in 1989 [194] tackled a much more difficult user scenario, where the goal was to examine the effects of relevance feedback. The 1987 system (with weak stemming and no spelling correction) was the base system, with a second system (qe) offering query expansion (look for books similar to), and a third system (full) which also included a "shelf browsing" system based on the Dewey class number order. For reasons related to the logistics of dealing with the data underlying the OPAC system, it was impossible to set up true operational testing, and a laboratory experiment with over 50 subjects was done instead. The task was to build reading lists for specific essay questions and the subjects were asked to use the base system for 15 minutes and then use either the qe or the full system (brief demonstrations of these systems were also done before use). The data for analysis was the transaction log and transcripts of recorded interviews. Based on the interviews, the qe (query expansion) system was considered highly acceptable, with the full system (shelf browsing) much less so. More than two-fifths of records based on query expansion were chosen by the users, with only one-fifth of those from the full system chosen.

Later in 1989 the Okapi system moved to the Centre for Interactive Systems Research at City University, London and a second set of experiments using relevance feedback was done [77, 195], this time within an operational setting using both the City catalogue and a section of the INSPEC database (computer science and information technology). A terminal with Okapi query expansion was available for six months, with searches logged and 120 user interviews done in the last three months. Query expansion was offered only when searchers had chosen at least two items as relevant; this happened in 43% of the logged searches and expansion was used in 31% of those searches, or about 13% of the total searches. For over half of the time it was used, no additional items were selected by the users. Post search interviews revealed that 41 out of the 45 users that did not use query expansion had found all the books they wanted already. However replays of those searches did show that there was indeed more to be found 50% of the time.

What were the results of these experiments? Clearly the best match ranked results from the first experiment were better than the Boolean results, although there could be little actual user analysis. The weak stemming made a small improvement in some searches, with the spelling correction helping in only a few. Relevance feedback worked well for the particular task chosen in the laboratory experiment, but was not heavily used in an operational setting. Note that these experiments were the first time that search methodologies proven in a batch mode were then evaluated in an operational setting (with the exception of the single CITE evaluation by NLM). As such they also illustrated the difficulties in transitioning (and then evaluating) these technologies to real world settings. The differences between two techniques have to be noticed by users, the specific tasks being examined have to "require" these new techniques, and the huge amount of noise involved in user studies (variations in users, topics, etc.) can often swamp any significant results. All of these issues have continued to plague user testing, as will be seen throughout the rest of this chapter.

In addition to these early user experiments, considerable discussion (and work) was being done in user modeling, in particular looking at the meaning of relevance, a concept that is central to evaluation of information retrieval. The batch experiments, starting back with Cranfield, all carefully defined relevance, and also made simplifying assumptions in order to operationalize the making of relevance judgements. These simple assumptions were criticized heavily, along with much theoretical discussion and some user experiments. One of the central figures looking at relevance was Tefko Saracevic, who started writing about relevance in the 1970s. A recent set of papers by him [153, 154] not only reviewed his work but surveyed other past work in relevance, both in the theoretical sense (the first paper), and in a review of the user studies (second paper).

Saracevic (and others) pointed out that the simplifying assumptions made about relevance in the batch evaluations did not reflect how users viewed relevance in the real world. The batch relevance judgments were based solely on topicality, they were usually binary, each document was considered independently, and it was assumed that judgments did not change over time (or across users). This was not meant just as a criticism of the batch evaluations (which clearly were doing useful research), but as a spur to further user experiments to better understand how users actually viewed relevance. Saracevic [154] then described various user studies that had been done to examine each of these assumptions.

Additionally he summarized a series of studies that looked at various relevance criteria, divided into the following categories:

- Content: topic quality, depth, scope, currency, treatment, clarity

- Object: characteristics of information objects, e.g., type, organization, representation, format, availability, accessibility, costs

- Validity: accuracy of information provided, authority, trustworthiness of sources, verifiability

- Use or situational match: appropriateness to situation or tasks, usability; value in use

- Cognitive match: understanding, novelty, mental effort

- Affective match: emotional responses to information, fun, frustration, uncertainty

- Belief match: personal credence given to information, confidence

These relevance criteria illustrate the huge variation that can be seen in how users approach information seeking, and in how they judge/value what is found. This variation continues to widen as information seeking has migrated from the simple OPACs to the vast amount of information available both on the web and through various social media such as Facebook. It is further multiplied by the explosion in the number and characteristics of users (far beyond the graduate student populations usually recruited for user studies!!).

## 3.3    INTERACTIVE EVALUATION IN TREC

Whereas TREC started in 1992 as a batch evaluation program only, there was always interactive involvement because the results were allowed to be created manually in addition to automatically (the creation method needed to be declared). By TREC-3 this was also formalized into an interactive track, where the 50 routing topics were used with the goal of creating the optimal routing query. There were four groups that took part, with results showing that humans could not beat the automatic machine learning methods used in routing (or conversely that the machine learning methods were indeed very powerful), but more importantly how difficult it was to evaluate interactive methods in the same manner as batch methods. Some of this comes from the "normal" difficulty in evaluation of interactive systems, but use of the TREC methodology added major problems, including the issues of which results to select for submission and how to deal with the natural disagreement between the "users" and the TREC relevance assessors. For an excellent summary of these problems (and the TREC interactive track in general), see [67], and for more on the various individual results, see both the individual online TREC proceedings and a special issue of Information Processing and Management [94].

The TREC-4 interactive track was more specifically designed for the interactive research community, with 25 of the ad hoc topics being used and two tasks created (find and save the most relevant documents in 30 minutes or create the "best" final query). This helped avoid some of the earlier problems but still left the issue of how to deal with the relevance assessment differences. Nonetheless 10 groups took part, including three commercial search engines, exploring such areas as graphical interfaces, visualization, etc. These papers (included in the TREC-4 proceedings) serve as interesting examples of user studies because they share the common thread of the same task(s). Additionally TREC-4 emphasized the analysis of the data and the search process by specifying what kinds of data should be collected, such as search logs, timings, use of various search features, etc.

Despite this general success, the interactive research community wanted better ways of comparing their systems within a task that was realistic for interactive searching. The TREC-5 task was done on yet fewer topics (12 old ad hoc ones), but with the goal of finding relevant documents that cover different "aspects" of the topic. The evaluation of the TREC-5 interactive track was separate from the main ad hoc task, with a different pool created from all of the documents submitted for the aspectual task. This pool was used to create lists of unique aspects for each topic, including which documents contained these aspects, and interactive groups were scored against these lists. Systems were asked to submit detailed event logging, including query terms, documents judged relevant, etc. and a detailed narrative account for one search, as once again the emphasis was on the search process. TREC-5 also featured a new experimental design [113] to allow direct comparison of results across participating sites. The twelve topics were divided into four blocks, and a common control system (NIST ZPRISE) was provided. Participating groups also tested their own system and the common experimental design dictated the order of the topics/systems to be searched. The goal was to be able to compare the systems by measuring users' performance on the common control system and on the site's experimental system. Only two groups took part in TREC-5, but the same task (with only six topics) was done by nine systems in TREC-6. An analysis of variance model was used to study the effects of the topics, the users, the systems and the various interactions [113]. It was found that there were significant effects from all three factors, with the topic effects being the largest.

Note that whereas the TREC-6 effort represented the first true interactive cross-site comparison, several issues remained troublesome. There were doubts as to whether the common control system method fully removed site-related differences, with a few attempts made to validate this [170]. Equally important, there were serious concerns about the logistic requirements both to "waste" time on an "uninteresting" control system and to use so few topics (given the known heavy effects of topic differences). For these reasons, the common control system was dropped for TREC-7, with each of the eight participating sites substituting a control system of their own, but keeping the common experimental design. Although this did not allow strict comparison across systems, it did allow each site to make a clean comparison to their own control system (unfortunately the differences were generally nonsignificant). The aspectual task was continued, with eight ad hoc topics specifically tailored for aspectual retrieval. The measures used were aspectual recall, aspectual precision, and elapsed time for the search. TREC-8 continued the same task, for six topics and seven sites, with generally the same evaluation issues. It is important to note that whereas the evaluation issues remained the same, each of these TRECs provided a common task and common measures that allowed interesting user studies to take place and to be informally compared among the systems. TREC-9 focused on a question-answering task, with eight challenging questions that users had to answer in five minutes, including providing the supporting answer document. The scoring was based on getting an answer plus the elapsed time. Five minutes was probably too short for this task for some topics , but again there were interesting and useful results from this task.

For TREC-10 it was decided to emphasize observational studies as opposed to system comparisons, with the goal of defining a new task for TREC-11. The public web was the data to be searched, and a common focus was provided by picking four search tasks (finding medical information, shopping, travel planning, and research for a paper), with eight topics spread across these areas. This general task was continued in TREC-11, this time using the TREC gov collection rather than the public web. An optional common search engine (Panoptic) was provided, with the task sharpened to require either short answers or a good web site for the answers. Additionally the experimental design developed earlier for TREC-6 was used, again allowing for within-system comparison of results. This task was continued in TREC-12 as a subset of the main web track, where the task was topic distillation and eight of the web topics were modified for better interactive searching.

TREC-12 (2003) marked the end of the formal interactive track in TREC. Just as the batch-oriented TREC ad hoc tasks and test collections had been useful in improving the underlying search engines, the TREC interactive track came along at a time when user studies were migrating from the limited OPAC system work to the much larger web. In addition to all of the results from the user studies, much was learned about what kinds of (TREC) tasks were most useful for system comparison, what measures were informative, and what kinds of common data were interesting to collect. Additionally a control system/experimental design methodology was developed, modified, and thoroughly tested. However there was disappointment in the general failure to detect significant differences between methodologies. Dumais [67] concluded her comments on the track by saying "It is always difficult to interpret the failure to find significant effects–it could mean that there are no effects or that there is still sufficiently high variability, making it difficult to detect all but the strongest effects. The continuing, strong desire for more experimental power to find significant effects, when they exist, requires a reduction in the variability or an increase in the number of searches. This might be accomplished by either increasing the number of tasks per searcher or focusing on subtasks."

Because of the logistics and expense of adding more tasks or searchers, the interactive community in TREC chose to move to a specific subtask. In particular the track looked at the effects of having more metadata about the user or topic, including the use of simple interactions, in order to improve early precision results (the High Accuracy Retrieval from Documents or HARD track). The participating groups first submitted their results based solely on the standard input topic (similar to the ad hoc task), but then had the opportunity to use additional information from the user (in this case the assessor who built the topic and also would make the final judgments). This information could take the form of metadata contained in the topic, or could be answers to a clarification form that the assessor completed. The second stage was then a submission of a new ranked list modified by the metadata and/or the interaction.

The 2003 HARD track should be considered a pilot, although interesting research was done in how to choose documents to submit for quick assessment (the simple interaction part). The 2004 HARD track [8] used 50 topics, all including metadata built into the initial topic. In addition to the standard TREC topic fields, there were new fields for *metadata-narrative*, explaining how the metadata is intended to be used, *retrieval-element*, specifying whether a full document or a passage was wanted, *familiarity*, *genre*, such as news-report, opinion-editorial, etc., *geography* (U.S. or not), *subject-domain*, *related-text.on.topic*, and *related-text.relevant*. The relevance judgments for the results were done at three grades: nonrelevant, hard relevant (relevant to topic and satisfies metadata), and soft relevant (relevant but does not satisfy metadata). Additionally if the granularity requested was at the passage level, then passage relevance judgments needed to be made (passages were defined by a document offset and their length). In addition to the metadata provided, the participants could submit a clarification form needing 3 minutes or less for completion (most groups used this form for quick judgments of keywords, documents or passages). In general the use of the metadata did not help results, often because the topics were such that the metadata did not provide useful additional information (a similar issue occurred in the elaborate TRECs 1 and 2 ad hoc topics). However some of the groups were able to obtain improved results using clarification forms. Note that several new metrics for passage retrieval were developed for this track [193] that were later used in the genomics track and in INEX.

The final running of the HARD track in 2005 had to be more constrained (no metadata and no passage judging) because of funding issues, however the clarification forms were continued and allowed to be more complex (but still only require three minutes to complete). Most systems were able to improve their baseline runs, but with a wide variation across topics as to which types of clarification worked best [9]. The HARD track morphed into a subtrack (ciQA) of the Question-Answering track in 2006 and 2007 [63]. The tasks in 2006 were similar to the HARD track, but here using the clarification forms for complex question-answering about relationships. The 2007 variation actually allowed the NIST assessors to interact with the participants' systems, with a limit of 5 minutes interaction time in which the participants could gather information. The basic goal of ciQA was the same as HARD in that groups hoped to get improvements in their baseline runs from these interactions. This did not happen consistently, partially due to some groups simply not using effective interactions, but also to problems with the task setup (assessors are not "naive" users after they have built a topic, had multiple interactions with clarification forms, etc.).

The final morph of the HARD track was as part of the current legal track. Starting in 2008, the interactive task [91] has used the Enron data and mirrored the actual legal discovery task where there is a "lead" attorney or topic authority who is the sole person who defines the task. There were 7 topics developed for this interactive task, and the participants were encouraged to interact with the topic authority (up to 10 hours worth of time) to clarify relevance issues, although other volunteer legal professionals made the relevance judgments (which could be appealed to the topic authority).

## 3.4   CASE STUDIES OF INTERACTIVE EVALUATION

TREC of course was not the only place where interactive evaluation was occurring; there were many other experiments. This section covers some of these, selected both to cover specific themes and to illustrate different issues/pitfalls in terms of higher level experimental design. They are organized by theme rather than chronologically.

The first theme is really a continuation of work done with the OPACs, i.e., do performance improvements seen in batch evaluations hold when tested interactively. There have been a series of papers dealing with this topic, in particular examining if the TREC batch system improvements resulted in improved performance for users. Hersh et al. [95] showed that better systems did lead to better interactive performance, however the differences were not statistically significant. This was quickly followed by a second paper (Turpin and Hersh [178]) investigating why this result occurred. Since the first paper used only six topics with 25 users and one task (the TREC-8 aspectual retrieval task), the second study also included the 8 questions from the TREC-9 question-answering task. Two different retrieval systems, a baseline system (tf*idf) and an "improved" system (Okapi), were set up using the same interface for each of the two tasks. There were 25 users for the TREC-8 instance task, who spent 20 minutes trying to find at least one document for as many aspects of the topic as possible. The experiment used appropriate randomization as to topics and systems and basically found that although the Okapi system had a 15% better instance recall, this only came from one of the topics out of the six. A second experiment was run using the TREC-9 question-answering task, with 25 users who had 5 minutes to find correct answers. This time the "improved" system actually had a slightly poorer performance (-6%).

A detailed analysis was then made to find out what was behind these results. Since the logs contained all the queries asked and documents found or saved, the researchers were able to trace how the systems performed with the actual user queries (instead of the TREC topics). They found that on average the users had indeed seen better results (precision at 10 was 55% higher, instances at 10 was 105% higher) with the Okapi system, and therefore could issue fewer queries. However, these improvements did not show in the final results because the users could find all the necessary relevant simply by issuing more queries. There was also a sufficient number of relevant documents available so that 30% to 55% of the relevant documents were not even read by the users. "It appears that the extra benefit of the improved system was ignored in the question-answering experiment and at best played a small part in the instance recall experiment" [178]. An unexpected complication was that the baseline system tended to retrieve shorter documents, therefore cutting reading time. However at least for these two tasks, users seemed able to do the task well with either system.

One of the issues with these two papers is that only a small number of topics were used. Whereas it is critical to have enough users in a study to detect significant differences in results, having a small number of topics makes generalization of the results difficult. This illustrates a major dilemma for interactive retrieval experiments, where logistics/expense usually force a choice between large numbers of users or large numbers of topics, even though the performance variation seen across topics is just as large (or larger) than the variation across users. Azzah Al-Maskari et al. [5] did a study with only 56 users but 56 TREC topics in a task to find as many relevant documents as possible in 7 minutes using two different systems. Because systems have a highly variable performance across topics, the systems in this experiment were selected differently for each topic. Given the results from three "comparable" systems for a given topic, the "good" system was the one with the best average precision and the "bad" the worst . Table 1 in their paper shows significant user performance differences in the time taken for the task, the number of relevant documents found, and user satisfaction, easiness, etc. between the good system and the bad. The second part of their experiment grouped the results into four topic sets based on the size of gaps in batch performance, and here they were able to show that as the performance gap grows smaller, so do the differences in user performance, with the gap needing to be at least 30% in order to see consistently better performance by users. Note that these experiments considered documents relevant only if the user judgments matched the TREC relevance judgments. If only user judgments were used (ignoring the TREC judgments), there were still significant differences with all 56 topics but these disappear when fewer topics were used.

A recent paper from SIGIR 2010 provides yet another experimental methodology for comparing batch results to user results. Sanderson et al [148] performed a crowd-sourcing experiment with 296 Turkers, who were shown paired results from the diversity experiment in the TREC 2009 ClueWeb track. Topics where ALL of the 19 runs in the diversity track had found two or fewer relevant documents were removed, leaving a total of 30 topics in test. The pairs of runs were selected from the 19 runs submitted to TREC by picking those runs with the same number of relevant in top 10 documents but a minimum difference in average nDCG of 0.1. The users were shown the top ten results (title, snippet and URL) and asked which set of results they preferred based on one of the subtopics of the full diversity topic (using the full topic had shown inconsistent results in pilot study). Each pairing was seen by an average of 8 Turkers and the votes were cumulative for each system of the pairs. The level of agreement between the votes and systems' nDCG performance was significant, even at smaller gaps.

It is obvious from this discussion that whereas conclusions vary as to whether batch improvements translate into user improvements, these conclusions are likely to be dependent on many factors in the experimental design. One factor is the number of topics examined; another is the gap in performance between the systems being compared. Maybe most critical are the specifics of the user task, such as the time allotted for task, the amount of interaction allowed, the instructions to the users, where the judgments come from (the batch experiment or the users' themselves), etc.

This leads into the second related theme and that is the general area of user modeling, where user modeling here means studying how a particular group of users behave as opposed to modeling a single user. These studies range from highly controlled laboratory studies where users are exposed to a minimum number of different variations to wide open observational studies, possibly even in an operational setting. The study by Kelly et al. [112] is an example of a very tightly controlled study. Her goal was not only to investigate how differences in system performance affect users, but also to develop an experimental methodology that could be used to isolate specific issues in how users actually search. She used a total of 81 subjects working with four topics from the TREC 2005 HARD track to investigate whether the ranking of the relevant documents or the total number of relevant documents in the top 10 ranks made a difference in users preferences of systems. The users searched each of the four topics on each of four "search engines" (this was appropriately randomized) and were asked to rank those engines based on their preferences. They entered a single query, read the titles and the documents and made relevance decisions. The four search engines were not actually search engines were ranked lists of documents in which the ranks or the number of the relevant and non-relevant documents were manipulated. For the first two studies, there were exactly five relevant and five non-relevant documents, but they were ranked from best (first five relevant seen first) to worst (relevant at ranks 6-10), with two intermediate cases. The third study had different numbers of relevant documents, ranging from 6 to 3, but controlled for order. The users were asked to vote their preferences after each search and could change these preferences after they had seen all four search engines (few did so). Note here that the relevant documents were carefully selected by the experimenter to be documents that would likely have a high-degree of agreement between the TREC assessors and the users (90% was observed). Detailed statistical analysis of the results showed that improved ranking resulted in significantly higher user preference, however the total number of relevant in the ranked list was more important than the ranking.

A study by Smith and Kantor [158] kept tight control on the "systems" but much less on the users because the goal was to observe more natural user behavior. There were 36 users who each completed 12 searches using either a standard system or one of two degraded ones. The standard system was the normal results of a Google search, with the other two being the same list but with degraded rankings. The CLR (consistently-low-ranking) one had the ranked list starting with those documents found at rank 300 and beyond, whereas the ILR one was inconsistent, with different starting points in the ranking for each query. All users searched on the same topics and were told there was a bonus for the person who found the most good information sources and the fewest bad sources. As queries were entered, the top 20 documents were displayed in the typical Google interface, but the links were disabled so that users had to make their decisions based on the titles, etc. The topics and users were carefully grouped into three blocks (appropriately balanced) to enable detailed statistical analysis of the results. The first and third blocks were searched using the standard (good) system, with the middle block using the two different degraded rankings. Users submitted their results to the researcher who graded each selected document as either a good, marginal or bad information source for the topic and the four evaluation measures were the average numbers for these counts plus the search time. The basic results show that users did just as well with the degraded systems as with the good ones by adapting their behavior, such as by issuing more queries (it takes less time to eliminate bad results) or by not resubmitting the same query to bad systems. Some of the same issues seen in the Turpin paper discussed earlier apply here, in that there could be many good sources in the good system, however by lessening the control of the users, more natural phenomena could be observed.

An example of an operational user study with minimal control is a 1992 study by Su [169] investigating what types of measures were correlated with user satisfaction. The 40 users (library patrons) were recruited as they came into the library to search for information. They then sat with one of six search intermediaries while the search was done (including paying the cost of the search), and were given or sent the set of documents retrieved in order to make relevance decisions. This represents a complete operational setting (at least in 1992). Almost 50% of the searches were for PhD research or other such high recall areas, with the rest being class assignments, grant proposals, etc. The complete search process was documented, including the time taken for the search, and the time to make relevance decisions, and there was a 60-minute interview asking the users about satisfaction, why they were satisfied, etc. Table 1 in the paper lists 20 different measures that were checked for correlation with satisfaction, with the highest correlation being the users' perception of the completeness of the search results (recall). In general precision was much less important, either because users were satisfied with only a few documents or because they were willing to look longer if they felt there were likely to be few relevant.

Another subject for user study involves investigation of how user groups tackle different search scenarios. Bhavnani [25] studied how domain specific knowledge affects searching, using 8 tasks adapted from the TREC 2001 interactive track (four tasks in healthcare and four in online shopping). His users were five healthcare search experts from medical libraries and four students who claimed three or more years of online shopping experience. This was an observational study, using think-alouds and interviews to collect the data. Analysis of these studies showed that the users employed different searching techniques when they were in their expert domain than when outside that domain, with generally better results in their domain. For example the shopping experts found cameras for $60 less than the healthcare experts, but the healthcare experts found the 9 categories of people needing flu shots by going to an average of 3.7 reliable sites whereas the shoppers went to 12 general purpose sites and none of them found all 9 categories. An important part of this study was to observe the searching process to determine the characteristics of domain specific searching. They found that both groups knew what types of websites to visit in their domain, including specific

URLS to search, and were also familiar with the internals of those sites so that they could efficiently and effectively search them. A log analysis study on this same topic is presented in the next section.

The final two studies presented on user modeling deal with comparing searching via social sources (such as friends, social networks), and searching with search engines. The two studies differ in the level of control but also in the goal of the study. Morris et al [124] did an informal experiment comparing using Facebook vs. using a search engine to find answers to an information need. The 12 participants brought their own search needs, most of which were relatively straight-forward requests for advice such as "Any tips for tiling a kitchen backsplash", or "Should I wait for ZuneHD or buy iPod touch (to gift someone)?". They then sent this request out to their Facebook friends (they needed to have at least 50 friends) and started their own searching. When they had finished searching, they checked with their Facebook network and captured a screenshot of the content and timestamps for any responses; this was repeated three days later. In general they got better information from the web, however social networking had added benefits, including sometimes different answers.

In contrast, Evans et al. [68] used two laboratory tasks, both of which were research questions about energy. Their questions were specifically picked not to be advice type questions, such as normally posted to Facebook, and were questions that are complex to search (one question was "What role does pyrolytic oil (or Pyrolysis) play in the debate over carbon emissions?"). Additionally they looked at all types of social search strategies, including calling or emailing friends, all the various social networking sites and other "socially-generated" sites such as question-answer sites, and blogs. They had 8 participants who worked in two blocks in a balanced experiment, with one block searching with social methods and the second using traditional search engines, databases, and Wikipedia, but not any of the "social" sites. There were semi-structured interviews, followed by detailed analysis of the various strategies that were used. One of their findings was that the results were very topic dependent, with the highly technical topics generally doing less well for social search strategies.

The last theme in this section is a continued look at relevance and the characteristics of relevant documents. The earlier work had begun looking at end users in libraries, but the information seeking tasks today are much broader. Barry and Schamber [21] compared two user studies that had the goal of finding relevance criteria. A more traditional one was done with 18 faculty and students who submitted a request for an online search and when presented with results (including full text documents, abstracts, citations, etc.) were instructed "to mark any portion of the materials that indicated something the respondent would or would not pursue." This was followed by open-ended interviews to collect various relevance criteria (989 responses to 242 documents). The other study was done within a specific domain with 30 users of weather information in areas such as construction, electric power utilities and aviation. In this case the information would be used to make planning decisions and they were asked to create time-lines of information seeking events leading to these decisions. The study interview then looked at three of these events, with the participants asked to evaluate the sources and presentation modes of these sources. In this case the "criteria were operationalized as ways in which sources or presentations made a difference to respondents in their situations." The study then looked at criteria that were common across the two studies, and ones that were different. The common ones were divided into ten categories:

- Depth/Scope/Specificity: extent to which information is in-depth or focused; is specific to the user's needs

- Accuracy/Validity: extent to which information is accurate, correct or valid

- Clarity: extent to which information is presented in a clear and well-organized manner

- Currency: extent to which the information is current, recent, timely, up-to-date

- Tangibility: extent to which information relates to real, tangible issues; definite; proven information is provided; hard data or actual numbers are provided

- Quality of sources: extent to which general standards of quality or specific qualities can be assumed based on the source providing the information; source is reputable, trusted, expert

- Accessibility: extent to which some effort is required to obtain information; some cost is required to obtain information

- Availability of information sources: extent to which information or sources of information are available

- Verification: extent to which information is consistent with or supported by other information with the field

- Affectiveness: extent to which the user exhibits an affective or emotional response to information or sources of information; information or sources of information provide the user with pleasure, enjoyment or entertainment

Criteria that were different for each study "appear to be due to the differences in situational contexts and research task requirements: specifically, control for source type in the Barry study and control for topic in the Schamber study [21]".

Other studies have looked how relevance criteria have changed in the web searching arena. Tombros et al. [177] used three different tasks and asked 24 participants to indicate the features of the web pages that were important to them for relevance criteria. The researchers were interested not only in what web document features were used in assessments, but also how the different tasks affected that choice. There was no control on the searching (other than time), and a think-aloud process and questionnaires were used to capture information. All tasks were set within a search scenario and were of three types: a background search, a decision task, and a listing task. The pre-search questionnaires looked for familiarity with task topic, etc., while post-search questionnaires asked about the clearness and easiness of task and the participants' perception of the importance of certain aspects of the web pages they viewed (both positive and negative aspects). It was found that most useful aspect of the web sites was the text, including the content and the numbers (especially for the decision task), followed by titles/headings and query terms. Another important criteria was the perceived quality of the web site, including its scope/depth, authority/source and recency. There was a difference across tasks in the importance of some features including a limited use of pictures for task 1 (the background search), the increased use of numbers for task 2 (the decision task) and the increased use of links for tasks 1 and 2. "As far as the scope/depth feature is concerned, its increased use in a decision task is based on that users required enough information in pages (e.g., enough details about prices, specifications, guarantees, availability of speakers, etc.) in order to make an informed comparison of the available choices [177]."

A crowd-sourcing experiment [11] also looked at relevance criteria on the web, including e-commerce tasks. There were 83 needs taken from the most frequent queries in Yahoo Buzz and Amazon product searches for two weeks. Thirty-five of them were e-commerce searches, whereas forty-eight were classic needs looking for items such as IRS tax forms, government jobs, or health insurance. For each need, there were 17 available criteria, with eight of them adapted from the work by Barry and Schamber [21] and nine more added specifically for the e-commerce task. The experiment used crowd-sourcing (2450 results), asking Turkers to select one or more criteria for these needs. Figure 1 in that paper shows that accuracy and validity were most important for both sets of needs, with availability coming in next (higher for e-commerce as would be expected). Differences can be seen in the two tasks, with more importance for depth/scope in the non-ecommerce needs, and price/value more important in the e-commerce ones.

The user studies in this section differ in the amount of control being exerted during the experiment, and in the number of users/topics/tasks addressed in the study, with most of the groups preferring to study more users and fewer tasks. This decision allows tighter focus in the analysis, such as in the study by Tombros et al. with only three tasks, where they were able to observe how the different tasks affected relevancy decisions. Note that in this study, and also in the Bhavnani study on domain-specific searching, the details in the higher-level experimental design (such as what tasks to pick, what to observe, etc.) were critical in getting useful final results. The two crowd-sourcing studies were able to have many users, and therefore were able to have more confidence in their end results, but could be successful only because they carefully focused the tasks (and set up the crowd-sourcing correctly). It is also interesting to contrast the tightly controlled study by Kelly et al. with the Smith and Kantor one, with one being able to use tight control to learn "micro" analysis of how users evaluate ranking and the other able to observe how users adapt to badly ranked results. There is no "right" way to design experiments, including how much control to use, how to balance the number of users versus the number of tasks, etc., but the key to the success of these various studies is that they selected clear, highly-focused initial goals and then determined which issues were most important to control based on these goals.

## 3.5    INTERACTIVE EVALUATION USING LOG DATA

One way to study many users is with the log data collected by the various search engines (and other places). Unfortunately this data is not usually publicly available, however research being done within the search engine companies provides some interesting insights into web usage. This section looks at some of that research and at some of the issues in dealing with web logs. A valuable resource for this work is the recent tutorial by Dumais, Jeffries, Russell, Tang and Teevan ( `http://research.microsoft.com/en-us/um/people/sdumais/Logs-talk-HCIC-2010.pdf`). This tutorial starts with listing the advantages of log analysis, including that the users' actual behavior is recorded as opposed to being reported or recalled or being the subjective impressions from laboratory experiments. Additionally the large (huge) sample permits subdivision of the data to any level of resolution, allowing for very focused experimental design. The disadvantages of the log files is that they are not controlled, not annotated with "macro-events", and there is no method of understanding why some micro-event has happened. A big challenge also is that these logs are massive, requiring serious efforts in focusing the experiment, in cleaning the data, in partitioning the data, and in understanding and interpreting the results. The papers presented in this section serve as illustrations of how this can be done successfully.

One of the first issues in log analysis is to decide what basic events/measures/counts to track. A workshop at the 2003 SIGIR conference [66] looked into this issue and one of the results was a paper by Fox et al. [70] detailing methods of collecting and then using the implicit user behavior available in web logs. The paper starts with a description of the embedded add-in for the client that allowed detailed tracking of users. The goal of the study was to collect both explicit feedback and implicit feedback in order to allow correlation of the various measures, and 146 internal Microsoft employees volunteered for the 6 week study. Two types of explicit feedback were gathered, including asking about the "relevance" of each individual search result visited ("liked it", "interesting but need more information", "didn't like it", "didn't evaluate it") and session level evaluation ("is this a new search", and "what is your level of satisfaction with the old search"); both of these were handled by system prompts based on the user actions. Tables II and III in the paper list 30 different implicit measures/counts made at both the result level (time spent on page, scrolling count, time to first click, etc.) and session level (number of queries, number of results returned, end action, etc.). The rest of the paper deals with statistical methods to combine the implicit feedback to predict the explicit feedback, proving that appropriate combination methods outperform simple uses of the implicit measures.

The number of implicit measures and features that are collected, and the sophistication with which these features can be analyzed, has exploded since then, with recent papers displaying large (and different) samples of the features now used. One example is the Teevan et al. [175] paper investigating the diversity of information needs behind similar queries and looking for methods that could be created to aid users in getting better results from these "ambiguous" queries. This study used a large sample of 44,002 distinct queries, each input by at least 10 different people. The types of features examined include some that are based only on the query itself (such as query length, contains URL fragment or time of issuance), some that need the result sets (such as the clicks, the number of ODP (Open Directory Project) categories or the portion of the urls that end in ".com") and some that need multiple instances of the same query (such as the number of times the query has been issued, the average number of ads displayed or the average number of results). The paper discusses ways these features can be combined to create models that improve the results of these types of queries. For example, query length and the use of URL fragments in the query help distinguish between navigational queries and informational queries.

The use of click data was the subject of a workshop at the Second ACM International Conference on Web Search and Data Mining (WSDM 2009), where a large query log from Microsoft was made available to researchers (14.9 million entries from one month in 2006, including 6.62 million unique queries). One of the studies [54] using this data looked at how click data could be combined with data from other sources to identify "diverse" queries (similar to the ambiguous queries in the Teevan et al. paper). One of the measures used was click entropy, which measures the spread of search results that are clicked on by multiple issuers of the same query (higher click entropies mean that users clicked on many different results). This click entropy was measured across the collection, showing that queries with low entropy accounted for 80.2% of the queries and that 95% of these returned names of organizations. The researchers used a subset of the data (queries with 50 or more repetitions and with five or more clicks) to investigate the correlation between click entropy and various other clues to ambiguity. They found little correlation between the query terms having many word senses (such as measured by WordNet or Wikipedia) and click entropy, however there was a positive correlation between the size of a Wikipedia article and click entropy, indicating that high click entropy might indicate broad topics with a need for aspectual retrieval.

The tutorial on log analysis also discussed the need to properly partition the logs based on the particular goals of a given study, such as partitioning by language, by time, and by the type of device being used to access the web. The study by White et al. [197] looking at how domain expertise affects the way people search the web is an excellent example of careful data partitioning. They started with 900 million browser trails from 90 million search sessions collected over a three-month period. The search sessions were then partitioned (by automatically classifying the visited pages using the ODP) into sessions where the users had (mainly) searched in one of four domains (medicine, finance, legal and computer sciences). They then selected the target group of users from this subset as those who had viewed 100 or more pages in these domains and whose page views contained 1% or more of domain-related pages. However this set of users are not necessarily domain experts, and the last partition was to identify as experts those users in this set that had visited PubMed, online financial services, Westlaw, or the ACM Digital Library, noting that three of these cost money and are not liable to be used casually. Once the users had been divided into experts and non-experts, the various other features of searching could be correlated with the two groups, showing for example that experts searched longer, issued more queries and visited more pages in unique domains in a given session.

In addition to careful partitioning of the logs, often there also needs to be "cleaning" of those logs, such as removal of spam, robot visits, and allowances for anomalies such as data drops, capped values, or "censored" data. This is particularly important in studying patterns, such as the study by Adar et al. [2] on web revisitation patterns. The goal of this study was to characterize how people revisit web sites using a 5-week web interaction log, followed by a user survey to identify intent.

The log was filtered to include only users with data for over 7 days, and a series of "outliers" were cleaned from the data such as users in the top 1% of activity (measured in different ways) who were assumed to be robots or other "badly behaved" users. This still left 612,000 valid users, and their visits to 54,788 URLs became the basis of the revisitation study. These URLs were binned by different criteria such as number of unique visitors (4 bins), median per-user revisits (5 bins) and inter-arrival times for a total of 120 possible bins to examine for usage patterns. Interesting clusters could be seen in these patterns, such as fast revisits could be porn or spam sites, with slightly different patterns indicating shopping or reference sites, whereas "medium" revisits could mean portals such as bank pages or news pages. These various patterns were then verified by a user study with 20 volunteers who were tracked for some of these URLs and also surveyed on a small selection of their revisits.

This final section illustrates the power of log studies to pinpoint and verify user behavior. In each of the cases there was a clear focus before the experiment on specific goals and this provided the researcher with a "gameplan" to analyze the data. Because the experiments basically started with a specific problem to solve, it is likely that the results can then be incorporated into new systems for the commercial search engines.

CHAPTER 4

# Conclusion

## 4.1  INTRODUCTION

This lecture concludes with some thoughts on how to design an experiment, pulling together some of the ideas from earlier chapters. Additionally there is discussion of some very recent issues in evaluation, both in methodology and in metrics, and a personal look ahead at some future challenges.

## 4.2  SOME THOUGHTS ON HOW TO DESIGN AN EXPERIMENT

In 1992 Jean Tague-Sutcliffe wrote "The Pragmatics of Information Retrieval Experimentation, Revisited" [172], where revisited meant that she had written an earlier article for the Karen Spärck Jones 1981 book [167]. In the 1992 article she discussed the series of decisions that needed to be made before any experimentation could start, and most of these ideas are still valid almost 20 years later.

Her first decision was "To test or not to test", where she said "An experiment should have a purpose; it is a means to an end, not an end in itself. It is therefore essential that the investigator delineate clearly the purpose of the test, the addition to knowledge that will result from its execution, and ensure that this addition has not already been made." In these days of fast computers, readily available data such as the TREC data, and a push to publish, it is sometimes easy to forget this. But the most critical key to the success of an experiment is to have such a focused goal that the variables are "easy" to define and operationalize, it is "obvious" whether the experiment was a success or "failure" (either is OK), and the results can be presented in such a concise fashion that readers immediately understand what was learned. Note that this applies whether the experiment involves the study of search logs, an operational user study or using a test collection. The successful log studies discussed in Chapter 3 were strongly focused and therefore were able to draw conclusions, such as the one looking at the effects of domain expertise [197] from massive data files. The Medlars operational user study [115] had a clear goal even though it was necessarily less focused, and that goal drove the intricate design of the recall and precision databases to allow non-biased measurements of performance. TREC (and similar) evaluations are even less focused, with the data and the task defined, but the actual experiments up to the participants. Whereas this allows greater freedom, it also can lead to results where it is not clear what has been learned.

Another decision is how to operationalize the variables. The documents to be searched need to be identified, and the definition of a document for the particular experiment needs to be determined.

This may seem to be a simple task, however as information retrieval has branched beyond OPACs, the unit to be retrieved could be passages, blog threads, sections of video, etc. Again the goal of the experiment, and therefore the user application that is being modeled, *must* determine this. Evaluations such as INEX, TRECvid and the genomics track at TREC have done extensive work on this difficult problem.

Tague-Sutcliffe also discussed the issue of "information representation" because most of her documents were manually indexed. Whereas this does not seem to be a part of today's experimental scene, it is really a hidden variable. The search log experiments rely on many types of information, with new types continuing to be tried (see [175] for an excellent example of this). In test collection experiments the representation of the information may be encoded in the system, such as the use of language modeling, making it more difficult to understand the underlying effects of data.

The third variable Tague-Sutcliffe discussed was the users. Here she was looking particularly at user studies, and listed four types of categories:

- type of user –student, scientist, businessperson, child;

- context of user – occupational, educational, recreational;

- kinds of information needed – aid in understanding, define a problem, place a problem in context, design a strategy, complete a solution;

- immediacy of information need – immediate, current, future.

Note however that users are not just for user studies, they also are the basis of user models and therefore need to be considered as part of *all* experiments in the operationalization of other variables.

The fourth variable is the source (and format) of the user questions/queries/search statements. Here the user model is critical, determining not only the types of questions that are being used for testing, but also how those questions are collected/assembled/created. One of the important lessons learned in the CLEF cross-language evaluations was how to build questions that faithfully mirrored the way that native speakers would query in their language and also reflected the type of questions that might be asked within each language area [201]. Likewise the format of the questions needs to mimic how users might search within a given application; good examples here are the TRECvid questions and the work done with patents in NTCIR.

Another issue is how to measure the performance and how to analyze the data. This involves appropriate selection of metrics such that the user and the application will be cleanly modeled. It also includes (at least in this lecture) the choice of how to measure the correct answers or relevance judgments. These two issues are closely related, although not tightly coupled. For example the TREC ad hoc user model was a high recall user where relevance was taken to mean any document that could be useful in a report. Note that this would reasonably include "duplicate" information since an intelligence analyst (or a newspaper reporter) might well regard duplicate information as verification of some fact. It also meant that a document was either useful or not (relevant or not), implying binary judgments. Additionally the TREC ad hoc results were always considered ranked and therefore needed a recall/precision metric. However other high recall users could be patent examiners, where a single patent would invalidate the application. Here the judgments are again binary, but the metrics could be those used for known-item retrieval, such as the mean reciprocal rank (MMR).

High recall can also mean high recall of different aspects of a given search, such as finding books by a specific author or finding recipes. This user model occurred in the various TREC interactive tracks, where aspectual recall was used, and in the genomics track. It also was behind the diversity track for the web in which the goal was to identify the various subtopics of the query. The definition of relevant there was slightly changed, incorporating the novelty of the information. Other possible evaluations could incorporate the order the information is presented, the perceived validity of the source, or the currency of the information, in fact any of the relevance criteria discussed in Chapter 3. Some of these definitions of relevance will require different or multiple metrics, such as graded relevance metrics like nDCG (see [46] for an example).

Web searching is usually considered low recall, where the goal is to get the user something useful quickly. This leads to metrics like success@1, or nDCG measured at the top 10 or 20 documents retrieved. The search engines all use graded relevance judgments, often with five or more grades, implying that they consider these fine grades important to users. Another issue involving web search is the huge number of potential relevant documents and this scaling issue has led to new sampled pooling methods (requiring new metrics) in the recent TREC web tracks (see Chapter 2).

Finally there is the critical decision of how to analyze the data (and what to present to the readers). Large tables of recall/precision averages showing small differences from baselines are not very interesting, and one could question what is learned from that. Use of statistical testing can be done (see for example [97, 150, 159]) but has not been heavily adopted by the community. A personal preference would be to actually look at the data, examining issues like how many of the testing questions showed improvement vs. lack of improvement, how large that improvement was, and most importantly WHY this occurred. The Turpin and Hersh paper [178] exploring why user evaluations did not give the same results as batch evaluations is an excellent example of this, and the failure analyses done in some of the TREC research papers contribute more to understanding of the underlying issues of retrieval than these large tables of averages. However plans for this type of analysis need to be incorporated in the experimental design early on to ensure that appropriate data is collected.

## 4.3    SOME RECENT ISSUES IN EVALUATION OF INFORMATION RETRIEVAL

A brief survey of recent SIGIR and CIKM proceedings shows three main categories of current interest in evaluation. The first of these categories is deeper examination of the implications of current evaluation metrics and methodologies.

Robertson [135] analyzed the Geometric Mean Average Precision (GMAP) used in the TREC Robust track and noted that the difference between GMAP and MAP "has to do solely with emphasis on different parts of the effectiveness distribution over topics". In particular, the GMAP measure emphasizes improvements in topic scores where the initial score was close to zero, rather than giving equal emphasis to improvements across all the topic scores such as done by MAP. He expanded on this by adding that the use of these different methods of averaging (or indeed the use of different metrics) allow researchers to observe more clearly how their systems are operating (such as his comment that the use of relevance feedback becomes more questionable when measured using GMAP).

There have been several papers re-examining the use of statistical methods. Sanderson and Soboroff's poster at SIGIR 2007 [149] showed some problems with the use of Kendall's tau rank correlation method, where the issue was the dependency of the threshold on the range of scores in the set of runs being compared. Voorhees' poster at SIGIR 2009 [188] revisited the issue of how many topics are needed in order to show significant differences across systems. In this paper she noted that even with 50 topics, there will be a small number of results that will be falsely declared significant (well within the 5% probability of a Type I error) and that researchers should validate results on multiple test collections. A poster by Smucker et al. in SIGIR 2009 [159] compared different significance testing methods to investigate the effects of varying sample sizes on the results.

Another continuing topic for research is the quality/consistency of the relevance judgments and how this affects evaluation. This has been investigated starting back with the SMART system. Table 1 in a paper by Bailey et al. at SIGIR 2008 [16] not only summarizes this work but adds new observations comparing the CSIRO assessors (the gold standard) in the TREC 2007 Enterprise track to a silver standard group (science communicators outside of CSIRO) and TREC participants (the bronze standard), with the latter being shown as not as reliable. A recent paper by Carterette and Soboroff [44] used simulation to examine the effects of different types of assessors (optimist vs. pessimist) using the TREC Million Query collection; one of the goals of this paper was to speculate on possible problems using completely untrained assessors, such as in crowdsourcing.

A second category of recent evaluation papers involves better/easier ways of building test collections. Evaluations (such as in TREC) have shown problems with the very large collections, where it can be assumed that the judgments are not "complete" and therefore that the collection cannot be declared reliable in terms of reusability by systems very different from those used in building the pool. The Million Query track was started in TREC 2007 to investigate better ways to select documents for judging and Carterette et al. in SIGIR 2008 [43] presented an analysis of this work, concluding that it was more effective and efficient to judge fewer documents using more queries. A follow-on paper by Carterette et al. in SIGIR 2010 [42] looked at a methodology for designing reusable test collections at this large scale and then being able to validate (or not) their reusability.

Another way of dealing with incomplete judgments is to use metrics less sensitive to incompleteness. The bpref metric is one of these and He et al. in SIGIR 2008 [90] compared the use of different metrics (MAP, bpref, infAP and nDCG) in effectively training systems as the levels of completeness were varied (MAP was the least effective).

Test collections are very expensive to build, with the relevance judgments being the most costly. One option has always been to get participants in the evaluations to do the judgments, however this option has a mixed record in terms of dependability. Kazai et al. for the INEX evaluation tried a Book Explorer game [104] to gather assessments, investigating the use of incentives to entice players and to control for quality. The use of Amazon Mechanical Turk or other crowdsourcing platforms continues this work, with Alonso and Mizzaro's poster at SIGIR 2009 showing the use of Turkers to determine relevance criteria in e-commerce [11], and another paper [10] by the same group in a workshop at that conference asking if TREC assessors could be replaced by Turkers!! SIGIR 2010 had both a workshop entitled Crowdsourcing for Search Evaluation, and a paper by Sanderson et al. [148] using crowdsourcing to compare the effectiveness of different retrieval systems where Turkers voted their preferences of paired results.

The final category of recent evaluation papers involves better ways of "mirroring" the user in batch evaluations. Järvelin and Kekäläinen developed the nDCG metric [100] based on graded relevance judgments, and it has seen heavy use in commercial search engine evaluations. In 2008 Järvelin et al. extended the metric to handle sessions of multiple queries, clearly better modeling real user interactions with a system. This same theme has been continued in the TREC Sessions track started in 2010. Note that there has always been work on multi-query sessions in user studies, and also in the work with the search engine logs, however trying to simulate this in batch evaluations remains a challenge.

Another obvious poor modeling of users in batch evaluations are the simplistic relevance criteria generally used. The idea of novelty and diversity has inspired the diversity task in the TREC web track, and also a paper by Clarke et al. in SIGIR 2008 [46] proposing a framework for evaluation of novelty and diversity, including a new metric based on nDCG. Additionally there have been two recent workshops at SIGIR: "Beyond Binary Relevance: Preferences, Diversity, and Set-Level Judgments" at SIGIR 2008 and "Redundancy, Diversity, and Interdependent Document Relevance" at SIGIR 2009.

A paper by Turpin et al. [179] at SIGIR 2009 suggested that evaluations could better model users if they included summaries of the documents in the judgment process and suggested a metric suitable to accommodating this. Whereas work on sessions has concentrated on the multiple query aspect in batch evaluation, the process of deciding "where to click" has only be investigated in user studies. A workshop at SIGIR 2010 ( "Simulation of Interaction: Automated Evaluation of Interactive IR") further expanded on how users could be modeled for batch evaluation efforts.

The commercial search engine community has enormous amounts of logging data that can be exploited to better model users. Chapter 3 discusses some of the recent papers in this area. Additionally Radlinski and Craswell presented a paper at SIGIR 2010 [129] that examined the process of interleaving results from different search engines as a new way of evaluation without test collections. They showed that interleaving was better at detecting very small differences in retrieval effectiveness (note that small differences do add up) than a more traditional test collection methodology, at least at high precision tasks.

## 4.4    A PERSONAL LOOK AT SOME FUTURE CHALLENGES

Information retrieval has always placed a high importance on evaluation, and this has allowed great progress over the years in terms of improvements. However the downside of this is that areas that are difficult to evaluate tend not to attract much research. Therefore the development of new and different evaluation methodologies and metrics is a critical key to attacking future challenges. What follows is a discussion of four areas in information retrieval that hopefully will see more research in the future, given that there are better ways of evaluating them.

The first area is better understanding of how our retrieval processes/search engines actually work. The "Ideal" test collection proposed by Spärck Jones and van Rijsbergen [166] envisioned a series of different document types, different indexing schemes, etc., with the goal of seeing how the retrieval systems needed to be modified to deal with these differences. Although this collection was never built, current evidence from TREC and other evaluations tends to indicate that results from systems are fairly invariant to the domain and the type of textual documents (newspapers vs. medical documents vs. social science documents). The various indexing schemes (free vs. controlled terms vs. bibliographic information) have been mainly ignored in experimentation today. The requests now come in natural language from different users but have (unfortunately) never reached the 700 to 1000 they proposed. What might be useful to do today?

Experiments aimed at better understanding of our systems could be envisioned at two levels. The first level would be to investigate how the systems are working in the *simple* task of retrieval from newspapers, i.e., the TREC ad hoc task. Once this is better understood, a second level would look at how results would change as the systems move into truly diverse environments, such as different tasks, different types of documents (blogs vs. web vs. mixed media such as in the legal track in TREC), or different user populations.

For the first level we need better metrics and methodology for diagnostics. Robertson's analysis with GMAP [135] and his suggestion of using different metrics to tease apart system behavior is an example of working with metrics. The work with metrics likely needs to be tightly coupled with new diagnostic methodologies, however. A fruitful area for this investigation would be the causes of huge variations in system performance across topics, and there have been multiple papers trying to find ways of predicting performance on a given topic (for example [40, 62] and another lecture in this series "Estimating the Query Difficulty for Information Retrieval by David Carmel and Elad Yom-Tov").

Beyond predicting, however, a major source of improvement would be the ability to modify/tune the system on a per topic basis. This unfortunately turns out to be quite difficult; a 6-week workshop [83] in the summer of 2003 tried to determine the characteristics of topics (from the TREC ad hoc track) that would be helped by the use of relevance feedback, and could not reach any clear conclusions. The workshop employed eight of the best retrieval systems, along with their research teams, to do a series of controlled experiments with the TREC data *and* to do many hours of extensive failure analysis [31] using a specially-built tool. The results were often surprising and revealed just how complex the current systems are, with considerable interaction between the various (often minor) components of the systems (see for example [45]).

Another way to tackle the same problem would be to analyze the topic sets looking for patterns of interaction between systems and topics. An attempt was made to do this with statistics [18], again mostly revealing how complex the interactions are. Guiver et. al [75] showed that small sets of topics were able to predict system effectiveness, with those sets composed of different topics depending on how many topics were used. This implies that there *may* be some way of generalizing topic characteristics and *one day* being able to test more specific components.

The second area where more research is needed is better integration of users into batch evaluations. Chapter 3 illustrated the logistical difficulties of doing user studies at a large enough scale to deal with both topic variation and user variation issues. Small controlled studies are hard to generalize, however the mixed results from applying successful batch methodologies into user applications shows the importance of better understanding of how users interact with the systems. The commercial search engines are able to track, and often generalize, these interactions, but may have different goals in terms of how to apply their user models.

One possible approach would be a type of user simulation within a batch environment. This could start with large scale observations of users doing a simple, well-defined task. The goal would be to identify some specific issues that could then be modeled in a batch environment. Results of that modeling would then be user-tested as proof of "improvements". For example the TREC-3 interactive track task was to find as many relevant documents as possible in up to 30 minutes, with 25 topics being searched (by multiple users). There were 9 systems that tackled this task, usually trying different interfaces to "help" the users with the task. Suppose that from this user study it could have been observed that specific types of document surrogates (or document space representations) were better than others. This could then be further developed within a batch environment, with results brought back for user testing. This example may be too simplistic (or naive), however the goal of integrating the users into the batch process is too important to just ignore. Moving forward will call for both new evaluation methodologies and metrics. There is some promising recent work on user simulation, with a workshop at SIGIR 2010 [14], and the new Sessions track at TREC. This needs to be pushed by both the user study community and the batch evaluation community.

Another approach would be to take more advantage of the facts that we already know based on previous user studies. An example of this would be to try different categories of relevance. Saracevic [154] listed many criteria such as novelty, validity, usability, fun, etc. that could be the basis of research (and evaluation). Some work has been done in novelty, and the criteria of validity has been somewhat tackled in the web world by the use of links. Research on removing spam is also relevant here, at least as a part of usability. A second source for relevance criteria is the Alonso and Mizzaro [11] study on one type of web searching. A major barrier to research in these different versions of relevance is the evaluation in a batch mode, that is, how do we effectively model these criteria in test collections.

A third area for future research is better integration of information retrieval technology into other human language technology areas, or for that matter, into other related areas. The text retrieval part of information access is only one part of the information access process; other technologies such as machine translation, summarization, and speech recognition are also needed. Whereas TREC and other evaluations have worked across areas, such as with cross-language information retrieval, or the various question-answering projects, this is usually done by connecting components. There have been many instances of good question-answering components dealing with poor retrieval components, or poor machine translation components feeding into information retrieval components, but little research on true interactions of these components.

The NTCIR evaluation program has made several efforts in this area. One was the investigation of the effects of machine translation accuracy on patent retrieval [72], and another has been a deliberate linking up of the question-answering results to the retrieval results in the more recent NTCIR meetings. In both these cases, and in other such research, the goal has been to measure the effects rather than trying to better integrate the components. But suppose that it was known that specific machine translations (words) were poor, would it be useful to integrate that knowledge into the retrieval process? Maybe not as information retrieval seems rather tolerant of "errors" in documents, but if that translation involved a key word in the query, is there a way to avoid poor results, such as by trying multiple translations. As another example, results from poor retrieval can guarantee poor question-answering results, but can retrieval systems be more tightly coupled into question-answering systems to allow a true interaction, such as getting more documents if it is obvious that the answer has not been found (several groups have tried this with success). Certainly part of the problem is that each of these technologies have very distinct communities, with different training, different evaluation criteria, and often different publishing venues. One of the goals of the various evaluations that have spanned communities (such as the TREC speech retrieval, the CLEF and NTCIR cross-language retrieval and the multiple QA evaluations) has been to bring these communities together, but this has generally not led to better integration.

The same types of "non-interaction" occurs with other related areas, such as database technology and image retrieval technology. Effective use of metadata and work with semi-structured information would likely be helped by database technology. The various image and video retrieval challenges employ both image and text and speech, and here there has been more integration, with text seen as only one component of the retrieval process. It is not clear if this has happened because of the characteristics of the communities involved or because the evaluations have encouraged specific component evaluation by requiring runs using a single component for comparison. Maybe this type of evaluation can be tried with more success in other cross-community evaluations or maybe evaluations modeled after Spärck Jones's cascading evaluations [168] will emphasize the effects of the various components and encourage tighter integration.

The final area for suggested research in evaluation addresses a much broader issue. The OPACs and "plain text" retrievals that started our field have exploded in many directions. A look at the vast array of tasks supported by today's commercial search engines, such as e-commerce and people/URL location accessing, in addition to the standard "text retrieval", gives an idea of the breadth of challenges to retrieval (and evaluation). Add to this the multimedia aspect, such as working with maps, images, and video, and the social aspects such as Facebook, Twitter, and blogs and the prospect of evaluation becomes mind-boggling. And this is just the web; what about enterprise search, patent retrieval, medical data location, or legal e-discovery? How do we go about producing meaningful evaluations (or research) in this diverse environment?

One way is by targeting very specific tasks within a specific environment. The TREC tracks were formed to investigate specific issues in (plain text) retrieval, such as the robust track, but mostly to deal with these different environments, giving us the legal track, the genomics track, the enterprise track, etc. NTCIR, CLEF, INEX and FIRE have also taken this approach. This at least has allowed investigations into the issues in these different areas and has made some initial exploration of effective retrieval (and evaluation) strategies. Possibly this is all that can be done, and it is certainly useful as there are large potential audiences for this work.

But can we (or should we) try to learn more general principles about the retrieval process (including the user aspect of this process)? Are there commonalities across these tasks and applications that can be harnessed to improve retrieval in general or at least allow faster/better adaptation of systems to these diverse environments? A workshop (MINDS [38]) attempted to find some answers, and at a minimum laid out some of the challenges requiring research (and evaluation) that occur in most of these environments.

- heterogeneous data: spam, audio, video, slides, notes, images, metadata/structure
- heterogeneous context: diverse tasks such as finding, learning, monitoring, communicating, planning
- beyond the ranked list: information analysis and organization
- better understanding of what the user is actually doing

These are simply the challenges, not the answers, but it is critical that we as a community expand our research horizons, and necessarily our evaluation methodologies, to tackle today's world. This will not be easy; the SIGIR 2009 "Workshop on The Future of IR Evaluation" had good discussions but as many different opinions as to what could be done as there were workshop attendees. But limiting the scope of research because our evaluation methodology is too restricted is not an option.

# Bibliography

[1] The Truth, the Whole Truth ... *American Documentation*, 6:56, 1955. Cited on page(s) 2

[2] Eytan Adar, Jaime Teevan, and Susan T. Dumais. Large Scale Analysis of Web Revisitation Patterns. *Proceedings of the Twenty-Sixth Annual SIGCHI Conference on Human Factors in Computing Systems*, pages 1197–1206, 2008. DOI: 10.1145/1357054.1357241 Cited on page(s) 74

[3] J. Aitchison and C.W. Cleverdon. A Report on a Test of the Index of Metallurgical Literature of Western Reserve University. Aslib Cranfield Research Project, Cranfield, England, 1963. Cited on page(s) 4

[4] T.M. Aitchison, A.M. Hall, K.H. Lavelle, and J.M. Tracy. Comparative Evaluation of Index Languages. Institute of Electrical Engineers, London, England, 1970. Cited on page(s) 22

[5] Azzah Al-Maskari, Mark Sanderson, and Paul Clough. The Good and the Bad System: Does the Test Collection Predict Users' Effectiveness. In *Proceedings of the 31st Annual International ACM SIGIR Conference on Research and Development in Information Retrieval*, pages 59–66, 2008. DOI: 10.1145/1390334.1390347 Cited on page(s) 67

[6] J. Allan, J. A. Aslam, V. Pavlu, E. Kanoulas, and B. Carterette. Million Query Track 2008 Overview. In *Proceedings of the Seventeenth Text REtrieval Conference (TREC 2008)*, 2008. Cited on page(s) 46

[7] J. Allan, B. Carterette, B. Dachev, J. A. Aslam, V. Pavlu, and E. Kanoulas. Million Query Track 2007 Overview. In *Proceedings of the Sixteenth Text REtrieval Conference (TREC 2007)*, pages 85–104, 2007. Cited on page(s) 45

[8] James Allan. The HARD Track overview of the TREC 2004 High Accuracy Retrieval from Documents. In *Proceedings of the Thirteenth Text REtrieval Conference (TREC 2004)*, pages 25–35, 2004. Cited on page(s) 65

[9] James Allan. The HARD Track overview of the TREC 2005 High Accuracy Retrieval from Documents. In *Proceedings of the Fourteenth Text REtrieval Conference (TREC 2005)*, pages 51–68, 2005. Cited on page(s) 65

[10] Omar Alonso and Stefano Mizzaro. Can We Get Rid of TREC Assessors. In *Proceedings of the SIGIR 2009 Workshop on the Future of IR Evaluation*, pages 15–16, 2009. Cited on page(s) 81

[11] Omar Alonso and Stefano Mizzaro. Relevance Criteria for E-Commerce: A Crowdsourcing-based Experimental Analysis. In *Proceedings of the 32nd Annual International ACM SIGIR Conference on Research and Development in Information Retrieval*, pages 760–761, 2009. DOI: 10.1145/1571941.1572115 Cited on page(s) 72, 81, 83

[12] Javed A. Aslam and Virgil Pavlu. A Practical Sampling Strategy for Efficient Retrieval Evaluation. Technical Report, College of Computer and Information Science, Northeastern University, 2007. Cited on page(s) 46

[13] Javed A. Aslam, Virgiliu Pavlu, and Emine Yilmaz. A Statistical Method for System Evaluation using Incomplete Judgments. In *Proceedings of the 29th Annual International ACM SIGIR Conference on Research and Development in Information Retrieval*, pages 541–548, 2006. DOI: 10.1145/1148170.1148263 Cited on page(s) 46

[14] Leif Azzopardi, Kalervo Järvelin, Jaap Kamp, and Mark D. Smucker. Report on the SIGIR 2010 Workshop on the Simulation of Interaction. *SIGIR Forum*, 44(2):35, 2010. DOI: 10.1145/1924475.1924484 Cited on page(s) 83

[15] Peter Bailey, Nick Craswell, and David Hawking. Engineering a Multi-Purpose Test Collection for Web Retrieval Experiments. *Information Processing and Management*, 39(6):853–871, 2003. DOI: 10.1016/S0306-4573(02)00084-5 Cited on page(s) 38, 54

[16] Peter Bailey, Nick Craswell, Ian Soboroff, Paul Thomas, Arjen P. de Vries, and Emine Yilmaz. Relevance Assessment: Are Judges Exchangeable and Does It Matter. In *Proceedings of the 31st Annual International ACM SIGIR Conference on Research and Development in Information Retrieval*, pages 667–674, 2008. DOI: 10.1145/1390334.1390447 Cited on page(s) 39, 80

[17] K. Balog, I. Soboroff, P. Thomas, Peter Bailey, Nick Craswell, , and A.P. de Vries. Overview of TREC 2008 Enterprise Track. In *Proceedings of the Seventeenth Text REtrieval Conference (TREC 2008)*, 2008. Cited on page(s) 39

[18] David Banks, Paul Over, and Nien-Fan Zhang. Blind Men and Elephants: Six Approaches to TREC Data. *Information Retrieval*, 1:7–34, 1999. DOI: 10.1023/A:1009984519381 Cited on page(s) 83

[19] F.H. Barker, D.C. Veal, and B.K. Gray. Retrieval Experiments based on Chemical Abstracts Condensates. Research report No. 2, UKCIS, Nottingham, England, 1974. Cited on page(s) 22

[20] J.R. Baron, D.D. Lewis, and D.W. Oard. TREC 2006 Legal Track Overview. In *Proceedings of the Fifteenth Text REtrieval Conference (TREC 2006)*, pages 79–98, 2006. Cited on page(s) 40, 41

[21] Carol L. Barry and Linda Schamber. Users' Criteria for Relevance Evaluation: A Cross-Situational Comparison. *Information Processing and Management*, 34(2/3):219–236, 1998. DOI: 10.1016/S0306-4573(97)00078-2 Cited on page(s) 70, 71, 72

[22] Nicholas Belkin. Anomalous States of Knowledge as a Basis for Information Retrieval. *The Canadian Journal of Information Science*, 5:133–143, 1980. Cited on page(s) 58

[23] N.J. Belkin, R.N. Oddy, and H.M. Brooks. Ask for Information Retrieval: Part II. Results of a Design Study. *Journal of Documentation*, 38:145–164, 1982. DOI: 10.1108/eb026726 Cited on page(s) 58, 59

[24] Yaniv Bernstein and Justin Zobel. Redundant Documents and Search Effectiveness. In *Proceedings of the 2005 ACM CIKM International Conference on Information and Knowledge Management*, pages 736–743, 2005. DOI: 10.1145/1099554.1099733 Cited on page(s) 53

[25] Suresh K. Bhavnani. Important Cognitive Components of Domain-Specific Search Knowledge. In *Proceedings of the Ninhth Text REtrieval Conference (TREC-9)*, pages 19–26, 2001. Cited on page(s) 69

[26] Abraham Bookstein. Relevance. *Journal of the American Society for Information Science*, pages 269–273, September 1979. Cited on page(s) 28

[27] Christine L. Borgman. Why are Online Catalogs Hard to Use? Lessons Learned from Information-Retrieval Studies. *Journal of the American Society for Information Science*, 37:387–400, 1986.
DOI: 10.1002/(SICI)1097-4571(198611)37:6%3C387::AID-ASI3%3E3.0.CO;2-8    Cited on page(s) 60

[28] Pia Borlund and Ian Ruthven. Evaluation of Interactive Information Retrieval Systems. *Information Processing and Management*, 44:1–142, 2008. DOI: 10.1016/j.ipm.2007.03.006 Cited on page(s) 57

[29] M. Braschler, P. Schäuble, and C. Peters. Cross-Language Information Retrieval (CLIR) Track Overview. In *Proceedings of the Eighth Text REtrieval Conference (TREC-8)*, pages 25–34, 2000. Cited on page(s) 37

[30] Martin Braschler. Clef 2002 – Overview of Results. In *Evaluation of Cross-Language Information Systems, the Third Workshop of the Cross-Language Forum*, pages 9–27. Springer LNCS 2785, 2003. DOI: 10.1007/978-3-540-45237-9_2 Cited on page(s) 49

[31] Chris Buckley. Why Current IR Engines Fail. *Information Retrieval*, 12(6):652–665, 2009. DOI: 10.1007/s10791-009-9103-2 Cited on page(s) 82

[32] Chris Buckley, Darrin Dimmick, Ian Soboroff, and Ellen M. Voorhees.  Bias and the Limits of Pooling.  In *Proceedings of the 29th Annual International ACM SIGIR Conference on Research and Development in Information Retrieval*, pages 619–620, 2006. DOI: 10.1145/1148170.1148284 Cited on page(s) 45

[33] Chris Buckley and Ellen Voorhees. Retrieval System Evaluation. In *TREC: Experiment and Evaluation in Information Retrieval*, chapter 3. The MIT Press, 2005. Cited on page(s) 34

[34] Chris Buckley and Ellen M. Voorhees. Evaluating Evaluation Measure Stability. In *Proceedings of the 23rd Annual International ACM SIGIR Conference on Research and Development in Information Retrieval*, pages 33–40, 2000. DOI: 10.1145/345508.345543 Cited on page(s) 32

[35] Chris Buckley and Ellen M. Voorhees. Retrieval Evaluation with Incomplete Information. In *Proceedings of the 27th Annual International ACM SIGIR Conference on Research and Development in Information Retrieval*, pages 25–32, 2004. DOI: 10.1145/1008992.1009000 Cited on page(s) 45

[36] Robert Burgin. Variations in Relevance Judgments and the Evaluation of Retrieval Performance. *Information Processing and Management*, 28(5):619–627, 1992. DOI: 10.1016/0306-4573(92)90031-T Cited on page(s) 28

[37] S. Buttcher, C.L.A. Clarke, and I. Soboroff. The TREC 2006 Terabyte Track. In *Proceedings of the Fifteenth Text REtrieval Conference (TREC 2006)*, pages 128–141, 2006.  Cited on page(s) 45

[38] Jamie Callan, James Allan, Charles L. A. Clarke, Susan Dumais, David A. Evans, Mark Sanderson, and ChengXiang Zhai.  Meeting of the MINDS: An Information Retrieval Research Agenda. *SIGIR Forum*, 41(2):25–34, 2007. DOI: 10.1145/1328964.1328967 Cited on page(s) 85

[39] B. Capps and M. Yin. The Effectiveness of Feedback Strategies on Collections of Differing Generality. In *Scientific Report ISR-18 to NSF*, chapter IX. Cornell University, Ithaca, N.Y, 1970. Cited on page(s) 15

[40] David Carmel, Elad Yom-Tov, Adam Darlow, and Dan Pelleg. What Makes a Query Difficult? In *Proceedings of the 29th Annual International ACM SIGIR Conference on Research and Development in Information Retrieval*, pages 390–397, 2006. DOI: 10.1145/1148170.1148238 Cited on page(s) 82

[41] Ben Carterette, James Allan, and Ramesh K. Sitaraman.  Minimal Test Collections for Retrieval Evaluation.  In *Proceedings of the 29th Annual International ACM SIGIR Conference on Research and Development in Information Retrieval*, pages 268–275, 2006. DOI: 10.1145/1148170.1148219 Cited on page(s) 46

[42] Ben Carterette, Evangelos Kanoulas, Virgiliu Pavlu, and Hui Fang. Reusable Test Collections through Experimental Design. In *Proceedings of the 33rd Annual International ACM SIGIR Conference on Research and Development in Information Retrieval*, pages 547–554, 2010. DOI: 10.1145/1835449.1835541 Cited on page(s) 80

[43] Ben Carterette, Virgiliu Pavlu, Evangelos Kanoulas, Javed A. Aslam, and James Allan. Evaluation over Thousands of Queries. In *Proceedings of the 31st Annual International ACM SIGIR Conference on Research and Development in Information Retrieval*, pages 651–658, 2008. DOI: 10.1145/1390334.1390445 Cited on page(s) 80

[44] Ben Carterette and Ian Soboroff. The Effect of Assessor Error on IR System Evaluation. In *Proceedings of the 33rd Annual International ACM SIGIR Conference on Research and Development in Information Retrieval*, pages 539–546, 2010. DOI: 10.1145/1835449.1835540 Cited on page(s) 80

[45] Charles L. A. Clarke, Gordon V. Cormack, Thomas R. Lynam, Chris Buckley, and Donna Harman. Swapping Documents and Terms. *Information Retrieval*, 12(6):680–694, 2009. DOI: 10.1007/s10791-009-9105-0 Cited on page(s) 83

[46] Charles L. A. Clarke, Maheedhar Kolla, Gordon V. Cormack, Olga Vechtomova, Azin Ashkan, Stefan Büttcher, and Ian MacKinnon. Novelty and Diversity in Information Retrieval Evaluation. In *Proceedings of the 31st Annual International ACM SIGIR Conference on Research and Development in Information Retrieval*, pages 659–666, 2008. DOI: 10.1145/1390334.1390446 Cited on page(s) 51, 79, 81

[47] C.L.A. Clarke, F. Scholer, and I. Soboroff. The TREC 2005 Terabyte Track. In *Proceedings of the Fourteenth Text REtrieval Conference (TREC 2005)*, pages 109–119, 2005. Cited on page(s) 45

[48] C.W. Cleverdon. Report on the First Stage of an Investigation into the Comparative Efficiency of Indexing Systems. Aslib Cranfield Research Project, Cranfield, England, 1960. Cited on page(s) 2

[49] C.W. Cleverdon. Report on the Testing and Analysis of an Investigation into the Comparative Efficiency of Indexing Systems. Aslib Cranfield Research Project, Cranfield, England, 1962. Cited on page(s) 2

[50] C.W. Cleverdon. The Effect of Variations in Relevance Assessments in Comparative Experimental Tests of Index Languages. Cranfield Library Report No. 3, Cranfield, England, 1970. Cited on page(s) 33

[51] C.W. Cleverdon and E.M. Keen. Factors Determining the Performance of Indexing Systems, Vol. 2: Test Results. Aslib Cranfield Research Project, Cranfield, England, 1966. Cited on page(s) 3, 8

[52] C.W. Cleverdon, J. Mills, and E.M. Keen. Factors Determining the Performance of Indexing Systems, Vol. 1: Design. Aslib Cranfield Research Project, Cranfield, England, 1966. Cited on page(s) 3, 7

[53] Cyril Cleverdon. The Signficance of the Cranfield Tests on Index Languages. In *Proceedings of the 14th Annual International ACM SIGIR Conference on Research and Development in Information Retrieval*, pages 3–12, 1991. DOI: 10.1145/122860.122861 Cited on page(s) 2

[54] Paul Clough, Mark Sanderson, Murad Adouammoh, Sergio Navarro, and Monica Paramita. Multiple Approaches to Analysing Query Diversity. In *Proceedings of the 32nd Annual International ACM SIGIR Conference on Research and Development in Information Retrieval*, pages 734–735, 2009. DOI: 10.1145/1571941.1572102 Cited on page(s) 74

[55] W.S. Cooper. Expected Search Length: A Single Measure of Retrieval Effectiveness Based on the Weak Ordering Action of Retrieval Systems. *American Documentation*, pages 30–41, January 1968. DOI: 10.1002/asi.5090190108 Cited on page(s) 25, 36

[56] W.S. Cooper. A Definition of Relevance for Information Retrieval. *Information Storage and Retrieval*, 7:19–37, 1971. DOI: 10.1016/0020-0271(71)90024-6 Cited on page(s) 28

[57] Gordon V. Cormack, Charles L. A. Clarke, Christopher R. Palmer, and Samuel S. L. To. Passage-based Refinement(MultiText Experiments for TREC-6). In *Proceedings of the Sixth Text REtrieval Conference (TREC-6)*, pages 303–320, 1998. Cited on page(s) 34

[58] G.V. Cormack. TREC 2007 Spam Track Overview. In *Proceedings of the Sixteenth Text REtrieval Conference (TREC 2007)*, pages 123–131, 2007. Cited on page(s) 43, 44

[59] Nick Craswell, A.P. de Vries, and Ian Soboroff. Overview of TREC 2005 Enterprise Track. In *Proceedings of the Fourteenth Text REtrieval Conference (TREC 2005)*, pages 17–24, 2005. Cited on page(s) 39

[60] Nick Craswell and David Hawking. Overview of TREC 2002 Web Track. In *Proceedings of the Eleventh Text REtrieval Conference (TREC 2002)*, 2002. Cited on page(s) 38

[61] Nick Craswell and David Hawking. Overview of TREC 2004 Web Track. In *Proceedings of the Thirteenth Text REtrieval Conference (TREC 2004)*, pages 89–97, 2004. Cited on page(s) 39

[62] S. Cronen-Townsend, Y. Zhou, and W.B. Croft. Predicting Query Performance. In *Proceedings of the 25th Annual International ACM SIGIR Conference on Research and Development in Information Retrieval*, pages 299–306, 2002. DOI: 10.1145/564376.564429 Cited on page(s) 82

[63] H.T. Dang, D.Kelly, and J.Lin. Overview of the TREC 2007 Question Answering Track. In *Proceedings of the Sixteenth Text REtrieval Conference (TREC 2007)*, pages 105–122, 2007. Cited on page(s) 43, 65

[64] Tamas E. Doszkocs. From Research to Application: the CITE Natural Language System. In *Research and Development in Information Retrieval*, pages 251–262, 1982. DOI: 10.1007/BFb0036350 Cited on page(s) 59

[65] Tamas E. Doszkocs and Barbara A. Rapp. Searching MEDLINE in English: a Prototype User Interface with Natural Language Query, Ranked Output, and Relevance Feedback. In *Proceedings of the 42nd Annual Meeting of the American Society for Information Science*, pages 131–139, 1979. Cited on page(s) 59

[66] Susan Dumais, Krisha Bharat, Thorsten Joachims, and Andreas Weigend. SIGIR 2003 Workshop Report: Implicit Measures of User Interests and Preferences. *SIGIR Forum*, pages 50–54, 2003. DOI: 10.1145/959258.959266 Cited on page(s) 73

[67] Susan T. Dumais and Nicholas J. Belkin. The TREC Interactive Tracks: Putting the User into Search. In *TREC: Experiment and Evaluation in Information Retrieval*, chapter 6. The MIT Press, 2005. Cited on page(s) 63, 64

[68] Brynn M. Evans, Sanjay Kairam, and Peter Pirolli. Do Your Friends Make You Smarter? an Analysis of Social Strategies in Online Information Seeking. *Information Processing and Management*, 46(6):679–692, 2010. DOI: 10.1016/j.ipm.2009.12.001 Cited on page(s) 70

[69] E. Fox. Characteristics of Two New Experimental Collections in Computer and Information Science Containing Textual and Bibliographic Concepts. Technical Report TR 83-561, Cornell University: Computing Science Department, 1983. Cited on page(s) 19

[70] Steve Fox, Kuldeep Karnawat, Mark Myland, Susan Dumais, and Thomas White. Evaluating Implicit Measures to Improve Web Search. *ACM Transactions on Information Systems*, 23(2):147–168, 2005. DOI: 10.1145/1059981.1059982 Cited on page(s) 73

[71] Atsushi Fujii, Makoto Iwayama, and Noriko Kando. Introduction to the special issue on patent processing. *Information Processing and Management*, 43:1149–1153, September 2007. DOI: 10.1016/j.ipm.2006.11.004 Cited on page(s) 48, 54

[72] Atsushi Fujii, Masao Utiyama, Mikio Yamamoto, and Takehito Utsuro. Evaluating Effects of Machine Translation Accuracy on Cross-Lingual Patent Retrieval. In *Proceedings of the 32nd Annual International ACM SIGIR Conference on Research and Development in Information Retrieval*, pages 674–675, 2009. DOI: 10.1145/1571941.1572072 Cited on page(s) 84

[73] J.S. Garofolo, C.G.P Auzanne, and E.M. Voorhees. The TREC Spoken Document Retrieval Track: A Success Story. In *Proceedings of the Eighth Text REtrieval Conference (TREC-8)*, pages 107–130, 2000. Cited on page(s) 36

[74] H. Gilbert and K. Sparck Jones. Statistical Bases of Relevance Assessment for the "Ideal" Information Retrieval Test Collection. British Library Research and Development Report 5481, Computer Laboratory, University of Cambridge, 1979. Cited on page(s) 25

[75] John Guiver, Stefano Mizzaro, and Stephen Robertson. A Few Good Topics: Experiments in Topic Set Reduction for Retrieval Evaluation. *ACM Transactions of Information Systems*, 27(4), 2009. DOI: 10.1145/1629096.1629099 Cited on page(s) 83

[76] D. Gull. Seven Years of Work on the Organisation of Materials in a Special Library. *American Documentation*, 7:320–329, 1956. DOI: 10.1002/asi.5090070408 Cited on page(s) 3

[77] Micheline Hancock-Beaulieu and Stephen Walker. An Evaluation of Automatic Query Expansion in an Online Library Catalogue. *Journal of Documentation*, 48(4):406–421, 1992. DOI: 10.1108/eb026906 Cited on page(s) 61

[78] Donna Harman. Overview of the Second Text REtrieval Conference (TREC-2). In *Proceedings of the Second Text REtrieval Conference (TREC-2)*, pages 1–20, 1994. DOI: 10.1016/0306-4573(94)00047-7 Cited on page(s) 32, 33

[79] Donna Harman. Overview of the Third Text REtrieval Conference (TREC-3). In *Overview of the Third Text REtrieval Conference (TREC-3) [Proceedings of TREC-3.]*, pages 1–20, 1995. Cited on page(s) 32

[80] Donna Harman. Overview of the Fourth Text REtrieval Conference (TREC-4). In *Proceedings of the Fourth Text REtrieval Conference (TREC-4)*, pages 1–23, 1996. Cited on page(s) 33

[81] Donna Harman. Overview of the TREC 2002 Novelty Track. In *Proceedings of the Eleventh Text REtrieval Conference (TREC 2002)*, pages 46–56, 2002. Cited on page(s) 53

[82] Donna Harman and Chris Buckley. Overview of the Reliable Information Access Workshop. *Information Retrieval*, 12(6):615–641, 2009. DOI: 10.1007/s10791-009-9101-4 Cited on page(s) 32

[83] Donna Harman and Chris Buckley. Overview of the Reliable Information Access Workshop. *Information Retrieval*, 12(6):615–641, 2009. DOI: 10.1007/s10791-009-9101-4 Cited on page(s) 82

[84] S.P Harter. The Cranfield II Relevance Assessments: a Critical Evaluation. *Library Quarterly*, 41:229–243, 1971. DOI: 10.1086/619960 Cited on page(s) 8

[85] Stephen P. Harter. Variations in Relevance Assessments and the Measurement of Retrieval Effectiveness. *Journal of the American Society for Information Science*, 47(1):37–49, 1996. DOI: 10.1002/(SICI)1097-4571(199601)47:1%3C37::AID-ASI4%3E3.3.CO;2-I Cited on page(s) 28

[86] David Hawking and Nick Craswell. Overview of TREC-7 Very Large Corpus Track. In *Proceedings of the Seventh Text REtrieval Conference (TREC-7)*, pages 91–106, 1999. Cited on page(s) 38

[87] David Hawking and Nick Craswell. The Very Large Collection and Web Track. In *TREC: Experiment and Evaluation in Information Retrieval*, chapter 9. The MIT Press, 2005. Cited on page(s) 38

[88] David Hawking and Paul Thistlewaite. Overview of TREC-6 Very Large Corpus Track. In *Proceedings of the Sixth Text REtrieval Conference (TREC-6)*, pages 93–107, 1998. Cited on page(s) 38

[89] David Hawking, Ellen Voorhees, and Nick Craswell. Overview of TREC-8 Web Track. In *Proceedings of the Eighth Text REtrieval Conference (TREC-8)*, pages 131–151, 2000. Cited on page(s) 38, 54

[90] Ben He, Craig Macdonald, and Iadh Ounis. Retrieval Sensitivity under Training using Different Measures. In *Proceedings of the 31st Annual International ACM SIGIR Conference on Research and Development in Information Retrieval*, pages 67–74, 2008. DOI: 10.1145/1390334.1390348 Cited on page(s) 80

[91] B. Hedin, S. Tomlinson, J.R. Baron, and D.W. Oard. Overview of the TREC 2009 Legal Track. In *Proceedings of the Einhteenth Text REtrieval Conference (TREC 2009)*, 2009. Cited on page(s) 41, 66

[92] W. Hersh, R.T. Bhupatiraju, L. Ross, A.M. Cohen, D.F. Kraemer, , P. Johnson, and M. Hearst. Overview of TREC 2005 Genomics Track. In *Proceedings of the Fourteenth Text REtrieval Conference (TREC 2005)*, pages 25–50, 2005. Cited on page(s) 40

[93] W. Hersh, A. Cohen, J. Yang, R.T. Bhupatiraju, P. Roberts, and M. Hearst. Overview of TREC 2004 Genomics Track. In *Proceedings of the Thirteenth Text REtrieval Conference (TREC 2004)*, pages 13–24, 2004. Cited on page(s) 40

[94] William Hersh. Interactivity at the Text Retrieval Conference (TREC). *Information Processing and Management*, 37(3):365–541, 2001. DOI: 10.1016/S0306-4573(00)00052-2 Cited on page(s) 63

[95] William Hersh, Andrew Turpin, Susan Price, Benjamin Chan, Dale Kraemer, Lynetta Sacherek, and Daniel Olsen. Do Batch and User Evaluations Give the Same Results. In *Proceedings of the 23rd Annual International ACM SIGIR Conference on Research and Development in Information Retrieval*, pages 17–24, 2000. DOI: 10.1145/345508.345539 Cited on page(s) 66

[96]  William Hersh and Ellen M. Voorhees. TREC Genomics Special Issue Overview. *Information Retrieval*, 12:1–15, 2009. DOI: 10.1007/s10791-008-9076-6 Cited on page(s) 40

[97]  David A. Hull. Stemming Algorithms: A Case Study for Detailed Evaluation. *Journal of the American Society for Information Science*, 47(1):70–84, 1996. DOI: 10.1002/(SICI)1097-4571(199601)47:1%3C70::AID-ASI7%3E3.3.CO;2-Q  Cited on page(s) 79

[98]  P. Ingwersen and K. Järvelin. *The Turn: Integration of Information Seeking and Retrieval in Context*. Springer, Dordrecht, The Netherlands, 2005. Cited on page(s) 57

[99]  Kalervo Järvelin and Jaana Kekäläinen. Ir Evaluation Methods for Retrieving Highly Relevant Documents. In *Proceedings of the 23rd Annual International ACM SIGIR Conference on Research and Development in Information Retrieval*, pages 41–48, 2000. DOI: 10.1145/345508.345545 Cited on page(s) 51, 53

[100]  Kalervo Järvelin and Jaana Kekäläinen. Cumulated Gain-Based Evaluation of IR Techniques. *ACM Trans. Inf. Syst.*, 20:422–446, October 2002. DOI: 10.1145/582415.582418  Cited on page(s) 51, 81

[101]  Kalervo Järvelin, Susan L. Price, Lois M. L. Delcambre, and Marianne Lykke Nielsen. Discounted Cumulated Gain Based Evaluation of Multiple-Query IR Sessions. In *Proceedings of the IR research, 30th European conference on Advances in information retrieval*, ECIR'08, pages 4–15, Berlin, Heidelberg, 2008. Springer-Verlag. DOI: 10.1007/978-3-540-78646-7_4 Cited on page(s) 51

[102]  Joseph John Rocchio Jr. Document Retrieval Systems – Optimization and Evaluation. Scientific Report ISR-10 to NSF, Cambridge, Massachusetts, 1966. Cited on page(s) 13

[103]  R.V. Katter. The Influence of Scale on Relevance Judgments. *Information Storage and Retrieval*, 4:1–11, 1968. DOI: 10.1016/0020-0271(68)90002-8 Cited on page(s) 28

[104]  Gabriella Kazai, Natasa Milic-Frayling, and Jamie Costello. Towards Methods for the Collective Gathering and Quality Control of Relevance Assessments. In *Proceedings of the 32nd Annual International ACM SIGIR Conference on Research and Development in Information Retrieval*, pages 452–459, 2009. DOI: 10.1145/1571941.1572019 Cited on page(s) 81

[105]  E. Michael Keen. The Aberystwyth Index Languages Test. *Journal of Documentation*, 29(41):1–35, 1973. DOI: 10.1108/eb026547 Cited on page(s) 58

[106]  E.M. Keen. Document Length. In *Scientific Report ISR-13 to NSF*, chapter V. Cornell University, Ithaca, N.Y, 1967. Cited on page(s) 16

[107]  E.M. Keen. Evaluation Parameters. In *Scientific Report ISR-13 to NSF*, chapter II. Cornell University, Ithaca, N.Y, 1967. Cited on page(s) 13

[108] E.M. Keen. Test Environment. In *Scientific Report ISR-13 to NSF*, chapter I. Cornell University, Ithaca, N.Y, 1967. Cited on page(s) 16

[109] E.M. Keen. On the Performance of Nine Printed Index Entry Types. British Library Report 5475, Aberystwyth, Wales, 1972. Cited on page(s) 58

[110] E.M. Keen and J.A. Digger. Report of an Information Science Index Languages Test. British Library Report 5120, Aberystwyth, Wales, 1972. Cited on page(s) 22

[111] Diane Kelly. Methods for Evaluating Interactive Information Retrieval Systems with Users. *Foundations and Trends in Information Retrieval*, 3:1–224, 2010. DOI: 10.1561/1500000012 Cited on page(s) 57, 58

[112] Diane Kelly, Xin Fu, and Chirag Shah. Effects of Postition and Number of Relevant Documents Retrieved on Users' Evaluations of System Performance. *ACM Transactions of Information Systems*, 28:1–29, 2010. DOI: 10.1145/1740592.1740597 Cited on page(s) 68

[113] Eric Lagergren and Paul Over. Comparing Interactive Information Retrieval Systems Across Sites: The TREC-6 Interactive Track Matrix Experiment. In *Proceedings of the 21st Annual International ACM SIGIR Conference on Research and Development in Information Retrieval*, pages 164–172, 1998. DOI: 10.1145/290941.290986 Cited on page(s) 63

[114] Mounia Lalmas and Anastasios Tombros. Evaluating XML Retrieval Effectiveness at INEX. *SIGIR Forum*, 41(1):40–57, 2007. DOI: 10.1145/1273221.1273225 Cited on page(s) 50

[115] F.W. Lancaster. Evaluation of the MEDLARS Demand Search Service. National Library of Medicine, Washington, D.C., 1968. Cited on page(s) 9, 10, 77

[116] M. Lesk, D. Harman, E. Fox, and C. Buckley. The SMART Lab Report. *SIGIR Forum*, pages 2–22, 1997. DOI: 10.1145/263868.263870 Cited on page(s) 11, 16, 18, 19, 20

[117] M.E. Lesk and G. Salton. Relevance Assessments and Retrieval System Evaluation. In *Scientific Report ISR-14 to NSF*, chapter III. Cornell University, Ithaca, N.Y, 1968. DOI: 10.1016/0020-0271(68)90029-6 Cited on page(s) 16, 18, 33

[118] David D. Lewis, Robert E. Schapire, James P. Callan, and Ron Papka. Training Algorithms for Linear Text Classifiers. In *Proceedings of the 19th Annual International ACM SIGIR Conference on Research and Development in Information Retrieval*, pages 298–306, 1996. DOI: 10.1145/243199.243277 Cited on page(s) 44

[119] H.P. Luhn. A Statistical Approach to Mechanized Encoding and Searching of Literary Information. *IBM Journal*, October:309–317, 1957. DOI: 10.1147/rd.14.0309 Cited on page(s) 11

[120] C. Macdonald, I.Ounis, and I. Soboroff. Overview of TREC 2009 Blog Track. In *Proceedings of the Einhteenth Text REtrieval Conference (TREC 2009)*, 2009. Cited on page(s) 42, 54

[121] R. Merchant, editor. *The Proceedings of the TIPSTER Text Program—Phase I*, 1994. Morgan Kaufmann Publishing Co. San Mateo, California. Cited on page(s) 27

[122] Donald Metzler, Jasmine Novak, Hang Cui, and Srihari Reddy. Building Enriched Document Representations using Aggregated Anchor Text. In *Proceedings of the 32nd Annual International ACM SIGIR Conference on Research and Development in Information Retrieval*, pages 219–226, 2009. DOI: 10.1145/1571941.1571981 Cited on page(s) 55

[123] Nathalie Mitev, Gillian Venner, and Stephen Walker. Designing an Online Public Acess Catalogue: Okapi, a catalogue on a local area network. Library and Information Research Report 39, London: British Library, 1985. Cited on page(s) 60

[124] Meredith Ringel Morris, Jaime Teevan, and Katrina Panovich. A Comparison of Information Seeking Using Search Engines and Social Networks. In *Proceedings of the Fourth International AAAI Conference on Weblogs and Social Media*, pages 291–294, 2010. Cited on page(s) 70

[125] E.M. Needham and K. Sparck Jones. KEYWORDS AND CLUMPS: Recent work on information retrieval at the Cambridge Language Research Unit. *Journal of Documentation*, 20(1):5–15, 1964. DOI: 10.1108/eb026337 Cited on page(s) 22

[126] I. Ounis, C. Macdonald, M. de Rijk, G. Mishne, and I. Soboroff. Overview of TREC 2006 Blog Track. In *Proceedings of the Fifteenth Text REtrieval Conference (TREC 2006)*, pages 17–31, 2006. Cited on page(s) 41

[127] I. Ounis, C. Macdonald, and I. Soboroff. Overview of TREC 2008 Blog Track. In *Proceedings of the Seventeenth Text REtrieval Conference (TREC 2008)*, 2008. Cited on page(s) 41

[128] J.W. Perry. Operational Criteria for Designing Information Retrieval Systems. *American Documentation*, 6:93–101, 1955. DOI: 10.1002/asi.5090060209 Cited on page(s) 7

[129] Filip Radlinski and Nick Craswell. Comparing the Sensitivity of Information Retrieval Metrics. In *Proceedings of the 33rd Annual International ACM SIGIR Conference on Research and Development in Information Retrieval*, pages 667–674, 2010. DOI: 10.1145/1835449.1835560 Cited on page(s) 81

[130] A.M. Rees. Evaluation of Information Systems and Services. In *Annual Review of Information Science and Technology*, chapter 3. Interscience, 1967. Cited on page(s) 8

[131] P.M. Roberts, A.M. Cohen, and W.R. Hersh. Tasks, Topics and Relevance Judging for the TREC Genomics Track: Five Years of Experience Evaluating Biomedical Text Information Retrieval Systems. *Information Retrieval*, 12:81–97, 2009. DOI: 10.1007/s10791-008-9072-x Cited on page(s) 40

[132] S. E. Robertson and M. M. Hancock-Beaulieu. On the Evaluation of IR Systems. *Information Processing and Management*, 28(4):457–466, 1992. DOI: 10.1016/0306-4573(92)90004-J Cited on page(s) 60

[133] S.E. Robertson. The Parametric Description of Retrieval Tests. *Journal of Documentation*, 25:1–27, 1969. DOI: 10.1108/eb026466 Cited on page(s) 26

[134] S.E. Robertson. On the history of evaluation in IR. *Journal of Information Science*, 34:439–456, 2008. DOI: 10.1177/0165551507086989 Cited on page(s) 1

[135] Stephen Robertson. On GMAP: and Other Tansformations. In *Proceedings of the 2006 ACM CIKM International Conference on Information and Knowledge Management*, pages 78–83, 2006. DOI: 10.1145/1183614.1183630 Cited on page(s) 79, 82

[136] Stephen Robertson and Jamie Callan. Routing and Filtering. In *TREC: Experiment and Evaluation in Information Retrieval*, chapter 5. The MIT Press, 2005. Cited on page(s) 44, 45

[137] G. Salton. Automatic Processing of Foreign Language Documents. In *Scientific Report ISR-16 to NSF*, chapter IV. Cornell University, Ithaca, N.Y, 1967. DOI: 10.3115/990403.990407 Cited on page(s) 18

[138] G. Salton. The "Generality" Effect and the Retrieval Evaluation for Large Collections. In *Scientific Report ISR-18 to NSF*, chapter II. Cornell University, Ithaca, N.Y, 1970. Cited on page(s) 15

[139] G. Salton. The "Generality" Effect and the Retrieval Evaluation for Large Collections. *Journal of the American Society for Information Science*, pages 11–22, January-February 1972. DOI: 10.1002/asi.4630230105 Cited on page(s) 15

[140] G. Salton. A New Comparison Between Conventional Indexing (Medlars) and Automatic Text Processing (SMART). In *Scientific Report ISR-21 to NSF*, chapter I. Cornell University, Ithaca, N.Y, 1972. Cited on page(s) 18

[141] G. Salton. A New Comparison Between Conventional Indexing (Medlars) and Automatic Text Processing (SMART). *Journal of the American Society for Information Science*, pages 75–84, March-April 1972. DOI: 10.1002/asi.4630230202 Cited on page(s) 18

[142] G. Salton and M.E. Lesk. Information Analysis and Dictionary Construction. In *Scientific Report ISR-11 to NSF*, chapter IV. Cornell University, Ithaca, N.Y, 1966. Cited on page(s) 16

[143] G. Salton and D.K. Williamson. A Comparison Between Manual and Automatic Indexing Methods. In *Scientific Report ISR-14 to NSF*, chapter VI. Cornell University, Ithaca, N.Y, 1968. DOI: 10.1002/asi.4630200109 Cited on page(s) 18

[144] G. Salton and C.S. Yang. On the Specification of Term Values in Automatic Indexing. *Journal of Documentation*, 29(4):351–372, 1973. DOI: 10.1108/eb026562 Cited on page(s) 19

[145] Gerard Salton. The Evaluation of Automatic Retrieval Procedures– Selected Test Results Using the SMART System. *American Documentation*, 16(3):209–222, 1965. DOI: 10.1002/asi.5090160308 Cited on page(s) 16

[146] Gerard Salton, editor. *The SMART Retrieval System*. Prentice-Hall, Englewood Cliffs, New Jersey, 1971. Cited on page(s) 11, 13, 15, 16, 18, 33

[147] Mark Sanderson. Test Collection Based Evaluation of Information Retrieval Systems. *Foundations and Trends in Information Retrieval*, 4:247–375, 2010. DOI: 10.1561/1500000009 Cited on page(s) 1, 7, 26, 32, 34, 51, 54, 55

[148] Mark Sanderson, Monica Lestari Paramita, Paul Clough, and Vanja Josifovski. Do User Preferences and Evaluation Measures Line Up. In *Proceedings of the 33rd Annual International ACM SIGIR Conference on Research and Development in Information Retrieval*, pages 555–562, 2010. DOI: 10.1145/1835449.1835542 Cited on page(s) 67, 81

[149] Mark Sanderson and Ian Soboroff. Problems with Kendall's tau. In *Proceedings of the 30th Annual International ACM SIGIR Conference on Research and Development in Information Retrieval*, pages 839–840, 2007. DOI: 10.1145/1277741.1277935 Cited on page(s) 80

[150] Mark Sanderson and Justin Zobel. Information Retrieval System Evaluation: Effort, Sensitivity and Reliability. In *Proceedings of the 28th Annual International ACM SIGIR Conference on Research and Development in Information Retrieval*, pages 162–169, 2005. DOI: 10.1145/1076034.1076064 Cited on page(s) 79

[151] Tefko Saracevic. Linking Research and Teaching. *American Documentation*, pages 398–403, October 1968. DOI: 10.1002/asi.5090190407 Cited on page(s) 20

[152] Tefko Saracevic. Selected Results from an Inquiry into Testing of Information Retrieval Systems. *Journal of the American Society for Information Science*, pages 126–139, March-April 1971. DOI: 10.1002/asi.4630220212 Cited on page(s) 20, 21

[153] Tefko Saracevic. Relevance: A Review of the Literature and a Framework for Thinking on the Notion in Information Science. Part II: Nature and Manifestations of Relevance. *Journal of the American Society for Information Science*, 58(13):1915–1933, 2007. DOI: 10.1002/asi.20682 Cited on page(s) 62

[154] Tefko Saracevic. Relevance: A Review of the Literature and a Framework for Thinking on the Notion in Information Science. Part III: Behavior and Effects of Relevance. *Journal of the American Society for Information Science*, 58(13):2126–2144, 2007. DOI: 10.1002/asi.20681 Cited on page(s) 62, 83

[155] Jacques Savoy. Stemming Strategies for European Languages. In *Proceedings of the 10th International Conference on Innovative Internet Community Services(IICS)*, pages 545–557, 2010. Cited on page(s) 49

[156] P. Sheridan, J.P. Ballerini, and P. Schäuble. Building a Large Multilingual Test Collection from Comparable News Documents. In *Cross-language Information Retrieval*, pages 137–180. Kluwer Academic Publishers, 1998. Cited on page(s) 37

[157] Elliot.R. Siegel, Karen Kameen, Sally.K. Sinn, and Frieda O. Weise. Research Strategy and Methods used to Conduct a Comparative Evaluation of Two Prototype Online Catalog Systems. In *Proceedings of the National Online Meeting*, pages 503–511, 1984. Cited on page(s) 59

[158] Catherine L. Smith and Paul B. Kantor. User Adaptation: Good Results from Poor Systems. In *Proceedings of the 31st Annual International ACM SIGIR Conference on Research and Development in Information Retrieval*, pages 147–154, 2008. DOI: 10.1145/1390334.1390362 Cited on page(s) 68

[159] Mark D. Smucker, James Allan, and Ben Carterette. Agreement Among Statistical Significance Tests for Information Retrieval Evaluation at Varying Sample Sizes. In *Proceedings of the 32nd Annual International ACM SIGIR Conference on Research and Development in Information Retrieval*, pages 630–631, 2009. DOI: 10.1145/1571941.1572050 Cited on page(s) 79, 80

[160] Cees Snoek and Marcel Worring. Multimodal Video Indexing: A Review of the State-of-the-art. *Multimedia Tools Appl.*, 25(1):5–35, 2005. DOI: 10.1023/B:MTAP.0000046380.27575.a5 Cited on page(s) 36

[161] Ian Soboroff and Stephen Robertson. Building a Filtering Test Collection for TREC 2002. In *Proceedings of the 26th Annual International ACM SIGIR Conference on Research and Development in Information Retrieval*, pages 243–250, 2003. DOI: 10.1145/860435.860481 Cited on page(s) 44

[162] E. Sormunen. Liberal Relevance Criteria of TREC—Counting on Negligible Documents? In *Proceedings of the 25th Annual International ACM SIGIR Conference on Research and Development in Information Retrieval*, pages 324–330, 2002. DOI: 10.1145/564376.564433 Cited on page(s) 53

[163] K. Sparck Jones. Collection Properties Influencing Automatic Term Classifications Performance. *Information Storage and Retrieval*, 9:499–513, 1973. DOI: 10.1016/0020-0271(73)90036-3 Cited on page(s) 22

[164] K. Sparck Jones and R.G. Bates. Report on a Design Study for the "Ideal" Information Retrieval Test Collection. British Library Research and Development Report 5488, Computer Laboratory, University of Cambridge, 1977. Cited on page(s) 23, 30

[165] K. Sparck Jones and D.M. Jackson. The Use of Automatically-Obtained Keyword Classifications for Information Retrieval. *Information Storage and Retrieval*, 5:175–201, 1970. DOI: 10.1016/0020-0271(70)90046-X Cited on page(s) 22

[166] K. Sparck Jones and C. van Rijsbergen. Report on the Need for and Provision of an "Ideal" Information Retrieval Test Collection. British Library Research and Development Report 5266, Computer Laboratory, University of Cambridge, 1975. Cited on page(s) 22, 82

[167] Karen Sparck Jones, editor. *Information Retrieval Experiment*. Butterworths, 1981. Cited on page(s) 1, 25, 26, 77

[168] Karen Sparck Jones. Towards Better NLP System Evaluation. In *Proceedings of the workshop on Human Language Technology*, pages 102–107, 1994. DOI: 10.3115/1075812.1075833 Cited on page(s) 84

[169] Louise T. Su. Evaluation Measures for Interactive Information Retrieval. *Information Processing and Management*, 28(4):503–516, 1992. DOI: 10.1016/0306-4573(92)90007-M Cited on page(s) 69

[170] Russell C. Swan and James Allan. Aspect Windows, 3-D Visualizations, and Indirect Comparisons of Information Retrieval Systems. In *Proceedings of the 21st Annual International ACM SIGIR Conference on Research and Development in Information Retrieval*, pages 173–181, 1998. DOI: 10.1145/290941.290987 Cited on page(s) 64

[171] D.R. Swanson. Some Unexplained Aspects of the Cranfield Tests of Indexing Language Performance. *Library Quarterly*, 41:223–228, 1971. DOI: 10.1086/619959 Cited on page(s) 8

[172] Jean Tague-Sutcliffe. The Pragmatics of Information Retrieval Experimentation, Revisited. *Information Processing and Management*, 28:467–490, 1992. DOI: 10.1016/0306-4573(92)90005-K Cited on page(s) 77

[173] Jean Tague-Sutcliffe and James Blustein. A Statistical Analysis of the TREC-3 Data. In *Overview of the Third Text REtrieval Conference (TREC-3) [Proceedings of TREC-3.]*, pages 385–398, 1995. Cited on page(s) 32

[174] Robert S. Taylor. Question-Negotiation and Information Seeking in Libraries. *College and Research Libraries*, 28:178–194, 1968. Cited on page(s) 58

[175] Jaime Teevan, Susan T. Dumais, and Dan Liebling. To Personalize or not to Personalize: Modeling Queries with Variation in User Intent. In *Proceedings of the 31st Annual International ACM SIGIR Conference on Research and Development in Information Retrieval*, pages 163–170, 2008. DOI: 10.1145/1390334.1390364 Cited on page(s) 56, 73, 78

[176] John E. Tolle. Monitoring and Evaluation of Information Systems Via Transaction Log Analysis. In *Research and Development in Information Retrieval*, pages 247–258, 1984. Cited on page(s) 59

[177] Anastasios Tombros, Ian Ruthven, and Joemon M. Jose. How Users Assess Web Pages for Information Seeking. *Journal of the American Society for Information Science*, 56(4):327–344, 2005. DOI: 10.1002/asi.20106 Cited on page(s) 71, 72

[178] Andrew Turpin and William Hersh. Why Batch and User Evaluations do not Give the Same Results. In *Proceedings of the 24th Annual International ACM SIGIR Conference on Research and Development in Information Retrieval*, pages 225–231, 2001. DOI: 10.1145/383952.383992 Cited on page(s) 66, 67, 79

[179] Andrew Turpin, Falk Scholer, Kalvero Järvelin, Mingfang Wu, and J. Shane Culpepper. Including Summaries in System Evaluation. In *Proceedings of the 32nd Annual International ACM SIGIR Conference on Research and Development in Information Retrieval*, pages 508–515, 2009. DOI: 10.1145/1571941.1572029 Cited on page(s) 81

[180] C.J. van Rijsbergen. *Information Retrieval*. Butterworths, 1975. Cited on page(s) 26

[181] P.K.T. Vaswani and J.B. Cameron. The National Physical Laboratory Experiments in Statistical Word Associations and their Use in Document Indexing and Retrieval. Publication 42, Division of Computer Science, National Physical Laboratory, Teddington, 1970. Cited on page(s) 22

[182] Ellen Voorhees. Question Answering in TREC. In *TREC: Experiment and Evaluation in Information Retrieval*, chapter 10. The MIT Press, 2005. DOI: 10.1145/502585.502679 Cited on page(s) 43

[183] Ellen Voorhees and John S. Garofolo. Retrieving Noisy Text. In *TREC: Experiment and Evaluation in Information Retrieval*, chapter 8. The MIT Press, 2005. Cited on page(s) 36, 51

[184] Ellen Voorhees and Donna Harman, editors. *TREC: Experiment and Evaluation in Information Retrieval*. The MIT Press, 2005. Cited on page(s) 27

[185] Ellen M. Voorhees. Variations in Relevance Judgments and the Measurement of Retrieval Effectiveness. *Information Processing and Management*, 36(5):697–716, 2000. DOI: 10.1016/S0306-4573(00)00010-8 Cited on page(s) 33

[186] Ellen M. Voorhees. Overview of the TREC 2002 Question Answering Track. In *Proceedings of the Eleventh Text REtrieval Conference (TREC 2002)*, pages 57–68, 2002. Cited on page(s) 42, 43

[187] Ellen M. Voorhees. Overview of TREC 2004 Robust Track. In *Proceedings of the Thirteenth Text REtrieval Conference (TREC 2004)*, pages 70–79, 2004. Cited on page(s) 51

[188] Ellen M. Voorhees. Topic Set Size Redux. In *SIGIR09*, pages 806–807, 2009. DOI: 10.1145/1571941.1572138 Cited on page(s) 54, 80

[189] Ellen M. Voorhees and Chris Buckley. The Effect of Topic Set Size on Retrieval Experiment Error. In *Proceedings of the 25th Annual International ACM SIGIR Conference on Research and Development in Information Retrieval*, pages 316–323, 2002. DOI: 10.1145/564376.564432 Cited on page(s) 32, 54

[190] Ellen M. Voorhees and H.T. Dang. Overview of the TREC 2005 Question Answering Track. In *Proceedings of the Fourteenth Text REtrieval Conference (TREC 2005)*, pages 69–80, 2005. Cited on page(s) 43

[191] Ellen M. Voorhees and Donna Harman. Overview of the Fifth Text REtrieval Conference (TREC-5). In *Proceedings of the Fifth Text REtrieval Conference (TREC-5)*, pages 1–28, 1997. Cited on page(s) 32, 36

[192] Ellen M. Voorhees and Dawn T. Tice. Building a Question Answering Test Collection. In *Proceedings of the 23rd Annual International ACM SIGIR Conference on Research and Development in Information Retrieval*, pages 200–207, 2000. DOI: 10.1145/345508.345577 Cited on page(s) 42, 43

[193] J.C. Wade and J. Allan. Passage Retrieval and Evaluation. Technical Report IR-396, CIIR, Department of Computer Science, University of Massachusetts, Amherst, 2005. Cited on page(s) 65

[194] Stephen Walker and Rachel de Vere. Improving Subject Retrieval in Online Catalogues: 2. relevance feedback and query expansion. British Library Research Paper 72, London: British Library, 1989. Cited on page(s) 61

[195] Stephen Walker and Micheline Hancock-Beaulieu. Okapi at City, an evaluation facility for interactive IR. British Library Research Report 6056, London: British Library, 1991. Cited on page(s) 61

[196] Stephen Walker and Richard M. Jones. Improving Subject Retrieval in Online Catalogues: 1. stemming, automatic spelling correction and cross-reference tables. British Library Research Paper 24, London: British Library, 1987. Cited on page(s) 60

[197] Ryen W.. White, Susan T. Dumais, and Jaime Teevan. Characterizing the Influence of Domain Expertise on Web Search Behavior. *Proceedings of the Second ACM International Conference on Web Search and Data Mining (WSDM 2009)*, 2009. DOI: 10.1145/1498759.1498819 Cited on page(s) 74, 77

[198] Ryen W. White and Dan Morris. Investigating the Querying and Browsing Behaviour of Advanced Search Engine Users. In *Proceedings of the 30th Annual International ACM SIGIR Conference on Research and Development in Information Retrieval*, pages 255–262, 2007. DOI: 10.1145/1277741.1277787 Cited on page(s) 55

[199] Ross Wilkinson. Effective Retrieval of Structured Documents. In *Proceedings of the 17th Annual International ACM SIGIR Conference on Research and Development in Information Retrieval*, pages 311–317, 1994. Cited on page(s) 53

[200] D. Williamson, R. Williamson, and M.E. Lesk. The Cornell Implementation of the SMART System. In *Scientific Report ISR-16 to NSF*, chapter I. Cornell University, Ithaca, N.Y, 1967. Cited on page(s) 15

[201] Christa Womser-Hacker. Multilingual Topic Generation within the CLEF 2001 Experiments. In *Evaluation of Cross-Language Information Systems, the Second Workshop of the Cross-Language Forum*, pages 389–393. Springer LNCS 2406, 2001. DOI: 10.1007/3-540-45691-0_36 Cited on page(s) 49, 54, 78

[202] Emine Yilmaz and Javed A. Aslam. Estimating Average Precision with Incomplete and Imperfect Judgments. In *Proceedings of the 2006 ACM CIKM International Conference on Information and Knowledge Management*, pages 102–111, 2006. DOI: 10.1145/1183614.1183633 Cited on page(s) 45

[203] Y. Zhang, J. Callan, and T. Minka. Novelty and Redundancy Detection in Adaptive Filtering. In *Proceedings of the 25th Annual International ACM SIGIR Conference on Research and Development in Information Retrieval*, pages 81–88, 2002. DOI: 10.1145/564376.564393 Cited on page(s) 53

[204] Justin Zobel. How Reliable are the Results of Large-Scale Information Retrieval Experiments. In *Proceedings of the 21st Annual International ACM SIGIR Conference on Research and Development in Information Retrieval*, pages 307–314, 1998. DOI: 10.1145/290941.291014 Cited on page(s) 32

# Author's Biography

## DONNA HARMAN

**Donna Harman** graduated from Cornell University as an Electrical Engineer, and started her career working with Professor Gerard Salton in the design and building of several test collections, including the first MEDLARS one. Later work was concerned with searching large volumes of data on relatively small computers, starting with building the IRX system at the National Library of Medicine in 1987, and then the Citator/PRISE system at the National Institute of Standards and Technology (NIST) in 1988. In 1990 she was asked by DARPA to put together a realistic test collection on the order of 2 gigabytes of text, and this test collection was used in the first Text REtrieval Conference (TREC). TREC is now in its 20th year, and along with its sister evaluations such as CLEF, NTCIR, INEX, and FIRE, serves as a major testing ground for information retrieval algorithms. She received the 1999 Strix Award from the U.K Institute of Information Scientists for this effort. Starting in 2000 she worked with Paul Over at NIST to form a new effort (DUC) to evaluate text summarization, which has now been folded into the Text Analysis Conference (TAC), providing evaluation for several areas in NLP.